A NOTE ON FRANCESCA BEAUMAN

FRANCESCA BEAUMAN ⬛⬛⬛⬛⬛⬛⬛⬛⬛⬛⬛⬛⬛⬛ e is the author of *The Pineapple: Ki*⬛⬛⬛⬛⬛⬛⬛⬛⬛⬛ *Ankle Preferr'd: A History of the Lonely F*⬛⬛⬛⬛⬛⬛⬛⬛ *Egg with One Hand: A Pocket Book for* ⬛⬛⬛⬛⬛⬛⬛⬛ *ime* between London and Los Angeles and is married with three young children.

BY THE SAME AUTHOR

The Pineapple: King of Fruits
The Woman's Book: Everything but the Kitchen Sink
Shapely Ankle Preferr'd: A History of the Lonely Hearts Advertisement
How to Crack an Egg with One Hand: A Pocket Book for the New Mother

HOW TO WEAR WHITE

A pocket book for the bride-to-be

FRANCESCA BEAUMAN

B L O O M S B U R Y

LONDON • NEW DELHI • NEW YORK • SYDNEY

First published in Great Britain 2013
This paperback edition published 2015

Copyright © 2013 by Francesca Beauman
Illustrations © 2013 by Victoria Sawdon
Graphs by John Gilkes

The moral right of the author has been asserted

Every reasonable effort has been made to trace copyright holders of
material reproduced in this book, but if any have been inadvertently
overlooked the publishers would be glad to hear from them.
For legal purposes the permissions acknowledgements on p. 201
constitute an extension of this copyright page

Bloomsbury Publishing, London, New Delhi, New York and Sydney
50 Bedford Square, London WC1B 3DP

Bloomsbury is a trademark of Bloomsbury Publishing Plc

A CIP catalogue record for this book is available from the British Library

ISBN 978 1 4088 4347 5

10 9 8 7 6 5 4 3 2 1

Typeset by Hewer Text UK Ltd, Edinburgh

Printed and Bound in Great Britain by CPI Group (UK) Ltd, Croydon CR0 4YY

MIX
Paper from
responsible sources
FSC® C020471

www.bloomsbury.com

CONTENTS

INTRODUCTION

I am a draper mad with love. I love you more than all the flannelette and calico, candlewick, dimity, crash and merino, tussore, cretonne, crepon, muslin, poplin, ticking and twill in the whole Cloth Hall of the world. I have come to take you away to my Emporium on the hill, where the change hums on wires. Throw away your little bedsocks and your Welsh wool knitted jacket, I will warm the sheets like an electric toaster, I will lie by your side like the Sunday roast.

WHETHER you have just received or just made a proposal of marriage, let us hope it lived up to Mog Edwards's to Myfanwy Price in Dylan Thomas's *Under Milk Wood* (1954). Now revel in the millisecond of peaceful, stress-free, pure happiness that is allocated to you before somebody, somewhere, bossily demands: 'So, have you set a date yet?' And so the Wedding Planning ('planning' — as though you're going in to battle!) begins, in a tornado of unwarranted advice, a tsunami of bossy directions and a storm of overly personal interrogation from those you hardly know and those you know oh-too-well.

Obviously a wedding is not just for you; if it were, most of us would choose to spend the entire occasion canoodling in a dark corner, giggling together at a lecherous uncle or a drunken aunt. But since you have been far too well brought up to behave in this fashion, your aim should instead be to balance other people's expectations with your own. While this may be easy in the beginning, it tends to become increasingly challenging in the run-up to the wedding, in particular during the stressful seven days or so before the Big Day itself, when it becomes all but compulsory to snap at a soon-to-be sister-in-law and moan about a once-was best friend. *How to Wear White: A Pocket Book for the Bride-to-be* hopes to offer an alternative perspective and, most importantly, a reminder to keep hold of your sense of humour.

This book also takes the not entirely fashionable stance that marriage itself is brilliant — an essential prerequisite for all of us who so boldly decide to take this huge leap of faith into a sixty-year-plus unknown. For many, whom you choose to marry will have more influence on your overall happiness, terrifyingly, than any single decision you will ever make in your life. As George Washington wrote to a friend in 1785, 'I have always considered marriage as the most interesting event of one's life, the foundation of happiness or misery.' This new job of yours — 'wife' — is a long-term gig, and there will be ups and downs, to say the least. Cling on to the fact that many couples do exist in a state of wedded bliss for many, many years; it is just that the reality of a happy marriage is rarely discussed, since the unhappy ones are *so* much more interesting.

However often people trumpet the demise of marriage, it still hasn't quite happened. Quite the opposite, in fact: in 2010 (the most recent year for which figures are available), the number of marriages in England and Wales increased by 3.7 per cent on the year before to 241,100. Simultaneously, almost the same number of books and magazines on the subject were published. The majority of these, though, were full of the sort of narrowly focused advice that, in the twenty-first century, has come to seem increasingly outdated. Wives today are widely expected to be able to discuss champagne consumption in the Yemen, quote Charles Darwin on marriage *and* save their husband from a heart attack during sex — ideally, all at the same time. This new role of yours thus demands a far broader skill set than ever before.

But fret not. *How to Wear White: A Pocket Book for the Bride-to-be* is here to help. Reflecting the full spectrum of this strange yet enduring institution, it aims to show that there is more to a wedding and, more importantly, to marriage than puffy dresses and wedding cakes. Contained within its pages is everything a twenty-first-century bride needs to know. Keep it stuffed inside your wedding garter or secreted beneath your bouquet, under your pillow or next to your home-made pickle collection. It might just keep you sane, and maybe — just maybe — your marriage happy.

ALL ABOUT CHAMPAGNE

Champagne is the only wine that leaves a woman
beautiful after drinking it.

Madame de Pompadour (Louis XV's mistress)

ACCORDING to the Office of National Statistics, we in the
UK spend over £5 million a week on champagne. No doubt a
large proportion of this is consumed by the newly engaged.
One of the best things about being engaged is that people buy
you champagne all the time. Or at least they should, and if the
bubbly is failing to materialize as often as you would like, then
the best course of action is to throw an engagement party at
once. This, by the way, is the only valid reason for an engagement party: really, how much attention does one woman
need?

The Romans were the first to plant grapes in the soil of the
Champagne region of France, probably around AD 5. The
area is physically very similar to the countryside south of Rome
known as Campania — hence the Latin origins of the word
'champagne'. This legendary liquid was originally conceived as
a red wine made from *pinot noir* grapes, pale pink in colour and
without any fizz. However, that part of France can get incredibly cold in winter, resulting in the premature halting of the
fermentation process, which leaves behind dormant yeast and
leftover sugar. When the weather warms up again in the spring,
fermentation restarts, releasing carbon dioxide into the bottle.
The result is bubbles — *lots* of bubbles, and sometimes so many
that the bottle explodes from the pressure. A bit like a bride
the week before her wedding, then.

From the time of the Romans onwards, thousands of hours were wasted attempting to eliminate all the bubbles from Champagne wine. A seventeenth-century Benedictine monk named Dom Perignon at the Abbey of Hautvillers is particularly well known for his efforts, and is often mistakenly credited with having invented champagne in the first instance: 'Come quickly! I am drinking the stars!' he merrily exclaimed on his first taste of this illustrious drink, or so the legend goes. Actually, he was trying to turn it back to conventional red wine. It was the British in the mid-seventeenth century who first spotted the potential appeal of this novel type of sparkling wine – not just because of the interesting taste, but also because the secondary fermentation process could be used to help preserve imported still wines. Champagne was a very different drink in those days, more like a dessert wine: it was extremely sweet, brownish-pink in colour and served icy cold. It was not long before the French caught on to its appeal, all the more so when the drink became a favourite of Philippe II, Regent of France from 1715 onwards.

The business of selling champagne in industrial quantities was always a woman's world. The first champagne house to produce it on a large scale was Veuve Clicquot (quickly followed by Bollinger in 1829, Krug in 1843 and Pommery in 1858), and this highly successful luxury brand is a fascinating one. Veuve (the French word for 'widow') Clicquot was born Barbe-Nicole Ponsardin in 1777 in Reims, the daughter of a textile manufacturer and politician. At the age of twenty-one she married François Clicquot, the son of another textile merchant, in a dark, underground cellar: religion had recently been abolished in France, making traditional church weddings illegal. François Clicquot, however, died just seven years later, and 'Widow' Clicquot immediately assumed control of his entire champagne business. In those days having one's husband pop his clogs had some advantages, it seems, allowing one the social freedom to live life the way one chose.

Within a few years, 'a bottle of the Widow' had become common parlance in European high society, as Widow Clicquot displayed her own kind of genius for promoting the brand. In 1814 came a particular stroke of luck: the Emperor Napoleon stayed with her in Reims on his triumphant return from exile on Elba. The story goes that she offered his officers champagne whilst they were still astride their horses, so they used their swords to take the necks off the bottles and in this way *sabrage* was invented. Whatever the truth of the incident, it was a huge boost to business.

Following the end of the Napoleonic Wars, Cliquot became the first champagne vendor to get her product into Russia: international trade remained illegal, but she boldly chartered a ship and persuaded her business partner to run the blockade with 10,000 bottles of her finest vintage. Demand for champagne in Russia was at fever pitch, and this secret advance shipment was an enormous financial success, selling out almost immediately. Even Tsar Alexander announced that he would in future drink nothing else. By the 1840s, Veuve Clicquot was selling over 400,000 bottles a year.

Veuve Clicquot died at the age of eighty-nine. While her legacy lives on at weddings everywhere (it is still her signature that is found on the Yellow Label bottles, Veuve Clicquot Ponsardin), she left behind few letters and no diary, and little is known of her. 'Anonymity runs in their blood,' Virginia Woolf wrote of Madame Clicquot and her sister, in spite of the fact that Cliquot was one of the first women to run an international commercial empire and the first ever celebrity businesswoman. Now, that's some trivia to use at your wedding

6

reception to kick-start the conversation at table twelve, or the 'odds and sods' table as it is sometimes known — you know, the one next to the flap in the marquee where staff bring out the food . . .

> The world is in perpetual motion, and we must invent the things of tomorrow. One must go before others, be determined and exacting, and let your intelligence direct your life. Act with audacity.
>
> Veuve Clicquot in a letter to her great-granddaughter

CHAMPAGNE EXPORTS

Pity the residents of Afghanistan: in the whole of 2013, fewer bottles of champagne were imported to the country than to anywhere else in the world. Who drank these precious twenty-four (24!) bottles, one wonders? Which extremely lucky souls? When it comes to these kinds of statistics, the devil really is in the detail.

	Number of 75cl bottles of champagne imported in 2013	Percentage change from 2012 to 2013
United Kingdom	30,786727	-5.1%
United States of America	17,853,267	0.9%
Germany	12,362,568	-1.6%
Japan	9,674,446	6.7%
Belgium	9,525,304	14.2%
Australia	6,023,165	11.4%
Italy	5,359,536	14.2%
Switzerland	5,137,664	-4.1%
Spain	3,066,022	-1.9%
Sweden	2,495,188	7.6%
The Netherlands	2,007,988	-12.7%
United Arab Emirates	1,689,447	12.1%
Canada	1,685,683	-0.8%

	Number of 75cl bottles of champagne imported in 2013	Percentage change from 2012 to 2013
Hong Kong	1,650,309	4.1%
China	1,633,146	-18.4%
Russia	1,539,299	4%
Martinique	1,402,769	12.6%
Singapore	1,358,769	-6, 5 %
Guadeloupe	1,341, 789	-9,8%
Austria	1,293,001	0.9%
Mexico	1,137,845	31.2%
Denmark	1,136,437	12.6%
Reunion	1,009,973	17.7%
Brazil	975,831	0.5%
Finland	891,324	1.2%
Norway	788,110	2.1%
Nigeria	750,169	-14.4%
Luxemburg	644,590	4.1%
Portugal	587,233	5.7%
South Africa	559,969	14.2%
Republic of Korea	557,131	4.7%
Ireland	415,604	-15.1%
New Caledonia	402,029	5.4%
New Zealand	387,827	25.6%
Qatar	370,345	16.4%
India	367,020	5.4%
French Guiana	360,309	30%
Czech Republic	331,629	-1.8%
Malaysia	328,559	23.4%
Taiwan	305,889	-8.5%
Poland	265,784	20.4%
Angola	252,923	79.3%
Greece	243,471	26.4%
Morocco	229,205	-0.6%
Congo	228,164	24.1%
Puerto Rico	211,791	16.9%
Gabon	208,052	6.7%
Thailand	201,108	-3.6%
Panama	200,326	9.3%
Ivory Coast	190,053	25.6%
Lebanon	186,977	-18%
Turkey	178,804	-5.9%
Cameroon	177,778	-2.8%

	Number of 75cl bottles of champagne imported in 2013	Percentage change from 2012 to 2013
Estonia	171,536	23.3%
Romania	162,291	-7.9%
Ghana	143,821	18.9%
Togo	143,231	2.6%
French Polynesia	136,585	-8.7%
Dominican Republic	127,358	20.5%
Ukraine	122,378	-25%
Mauritius	113,078	-20.7%
St Martin	111,369	-4.1%
Latvia	108,040	7%
Argentina	106,381	-4%
Lithuania	99,188	7.6%
Vietnam	98,603	10.1%
Philippines	95,795	6.7%
Maldives	90,908	23.2%
Indonesia	86,900	13.1%
Trinidad and Tobago	84,143	36.9%
Colombia	82,485	70.8%
Cyprus	78,119	-23.7%
Israel	75,727	4.9%
Barbados	75,605	43.4%
Malta	75,491	32.1%
Democratic Republic of Congo	71,869	-12.7%
Venezuela	63,973	7.7%
Macao	63,525	-20.4%
Chile	62,879	-20.5%
Benin	62,450	107.2%
Burkina Faso	62,278	44.7%
Georgia	60,929	11.6%
Kazakhstan	59,725	-7.3%
Croatia	59,367	-0.2%
Slovakia	58,857	18.7%
Andorra	53,981	-12%
St. Barts	53,273	-4.4%
Senegal	52,814	-10.9%
Hungary	50,657	20.2%
Bulgaria	49,594	25%
Bahamas	48,340	0.4%
Belarus	46,483	63.6%
Jersey	44,031	-22.4%

	Number of 75cl bottles of champagne imported in 2013	Percentage change from 2012 to 2013
Seychelles	39,661	13.4%
Equatorial Guinea	38,200	-35.7%
Ethiopia	37,053	13.6%
Paraguay	35,256	-61.8%
Peru	34,788	0.8%
Bermuda	32,869	-21.1%
Cayman Islands	32,452	-12.7%
Cambodia	31,645	64.2%
Algeria	31,490	-23.4%
Serbia	30,621	-8.9%
Haiti	28,118	-5.1%
Slovenia	27,584	4.3%
Iceland	27,475	17.1%
Uzbekistan	25,458	40.9%
St Martin	24,602	153.5%
Uruguay	24,182	-69.6%
Virgin Islands	21,856	-4.6%
Turks and Caicos Islands	21,590	28.9%
Egypt	20,808	45.2%
Jamaica	20,148	6.7%
Mayotte	18,540	28.3%
Kenya	18,251	10.2%
Montenegro	16,982	30.2%
Aruba	16,926	-38.7%
British Virgin Islands	16,492	10.3%
Costa Rica	16,184	48.2%
Sri Lanka	15,821	-30.9%
Guernsey	15,318	-44.4%
Tunisia	15,270	25.8%
Bahrain	12,464	-7.8%
Mongolia	11,631	-7.5%
Mali	11,266	67.1%
Madagascar	11,130	-40.4%
Bolivia	10,072	-6.2%
St Pierre and Miquelon	9,222	16.6%
Kyrgyzstan	8,934	14 790%
Surinam	8,923	-7.6%
Antigua and Barbuda	8,869	8.4%
St Lucia	8,412	27.6%
Jordan	7,914	-14%

	Number of 75cl bottles of champagne imported in 2013	Percentage change from 2012 to 2013
Albania	7,827	-32.4%
Guatemala	7,689	32.2%
Laos	7,544	23%
Gambia	7,260	3 261.1%
St Vincent and Grenadines	6,975	37.6%
Gibraltar	6,548	-1.9%
Canary Islands	6,275	131%
Djibouti	6,234	-6.6%
Bosnia Herzegovina	5,964	59.6%
Oman	5,952	-22.1%
Chad	5,829	-42%
Vanuatu	5,220	7%
Nicaragua	5,076	137.1%
Fiji	4,987	-2.2%
Curacao	3,988	77.5%
El Salvador	3,904	93.4%
Sierra Leone	3,864	-8%
Macedonia	3,525	48.7%
Ceuta	3,486	79.9%
San Marino	3,395	-29.1%
Democratic Republic of Korea	3,184	3 437.8%
Armenia	3,003	-53.4%
Liberia	2,690	170.1%
Grenada	2,616	189.1%
St Kitts and Nevis	2,550	43.3%
Lichtenstein	2,496	-17.4%
Niger	2,492	-60.4%
Guinea	2,183	-84.4%
Myanmar	2,173	-70.2%
Wallis and Futuna	2,046	-57.6%
Mauritania	1,901	-27.1%
Tanzania	1,866	-27.2%
Honduras	1,674	-41.6%
Azerbaijan	1,516	-78%
Ecuador	1,473	-80%
Iraq	1,368	-71.8%
Republic of Central Africa	1,239	-68.2%
Moldova	1,194	148.8%
Cuba	1,129	10.5%
Syria	888	2.8%

	Number of 75cl bottles of champagne imported in 2013	Percentage change from 2012 to 2013
Nepal	816	-22.3%
Greenland	579	374.6%
Anguilla	570	-65.1%
Cape Verde	546	-55.2%
Mozambique	546	-96.1%
Turkmenistan	522	443.8%
Zimbabwe	492	74.5%
Guyana	486	-6%
French Southern and Antarctic Lands	432	-10.7%
Iran	339	-48.2%
Bangladesh	330	175%
Guam	300	-67.3%
Belize	264	-65.4%
Uganda	252	-75.7%
Rwanda	252	-76%
Zambia	248	-60.8%
Eritrea	225	0
Bonaire, St Eustatius and Saba	186	0
Comoros	107	-73.6%
Guinea–Bissau	72	-89.7%
Tajikistan	42	0
Yemen	36	-35.7%
Sao Tome and Principe	30	-92.6%
Afghanistan	24	-80.0%

Source: Comité Champagne (CIVC)

THE FONT OF ALL WISDOM

IN the same way that shoes, wristwatches and ties tell you almost all you need to know about your date within a couple of seconds of meeting, the font you choose for your wedding invitation is also very revealing, not only about the two of you as a couple but indeed also as to the sort of shindig to which people are going to be turning up.

Classical 'script' fonts abound in this situation, and are almost guaranteed to be what the printer will recommend, as that is how people imagine wedding invitations to look – that is, how they look in films. Those for whom only embossing will do may find their options curtailed further still. When it comes to more home-made invitations, even boring old Microsoft Word has several acceptable 'script' choices (Kunstler or Vladimir, to name but two). And of course a quick Google search of 'classic wedding fonts' will produce literally hundreds of 'script' options.

However, it does not have to be thus. Demand more! Good taste is everything! Or, as the Irish aristocrat and revolutionary Lord Edward Fitzgerald put it, 'taste is the feminine of genius'.

Here are some other fonts you might consider if 'script'-style fonts fail to move you. Hopefully it is not even necessary to articulate that this list does not include the dreaded Comic Sans, which is without doubt the worst font ever invented. Just because it contains the word 'comic' does not render everything you write in it amusing. Quite the opposite, in fact.

ANTIQUE FONTS

Nothing adds a sense of occasion to the wedding like a beautiful old font. **Caslon Antique** has a nice eighteenth-century feel to it:

Good news! A wedding! Feasting and drinking Etc.

Century Modern looks like a nineteenth-century newspaper:

Attention all Wedding guests! Please
come and watch us marry each other.

ART DECO FONTS

Slightly more up-to-date but with a sense of permanence and style, these fonts go very well with that flapper dress you plan to wear. ODALISQUE is very *The Boyfriend*:

CRIKEY! POLLY AND JASPER ARE GETTING HITCHED!

More Arts and Crafts-y is something like Grasshopper:

Mr and Mrs Green invite you to the
wedding of their daughter.

MODERNIST FONTS

Never wacky, of course, but there's something about these more modern fonts with their clean and sans serif lines that adds an element of *Mad Men*-cool to your invitation, suggesting as they do a love of all things mid-century. **Neues Bauen** has a great Bauhaus feel:

> **Please join Otto and Lily for their upcoming nuptials and wurst-eating competition . . .**

Brandon Grotesque is an excellent, simple and clean contemporary font.

> We are getting married. Probably in a warehouse.

And if these all feel a little *de trop*, then of course good old **Gill Sans** is always an excellent standby.

BE STILL, MY BEATING HEART

IN the often-fraught weeks leading up to one's wedding, there tends to be an awful lot of chatter about one's heart. So let us establish exactly what it is we are dealing with here.

Origin of this oh-so-revered organ: The heart is the first functional organ; it grows out of embryonic cells that appear following gastrulation, which is one of the very earliest states of the embryonic development that follows the fertilization of an egg by sperm. The developmental biologist Lewis Wolpert once commented, 'It is not birth, marriage, or death, but gastrulation, which is truly the most important time in your life.'

Raison d'être: The heart is the muscle that pumps blood filled with oxygen and nutrients to all the body tissues. *Mais bien sûr.*

Size: About the same as a clenched fist.

Weight: About 10 or 11 ounces.

Location: Inside the ribcage, behind the breastbone, above the diaphragm and in between the lungs, in a moist chamber known as the pericardial cavity.

Structure: Four chambers. The top two, the atria, are where the blood is received from the rest of the body (*atrium* is Latin for 'entrance hall'); the bottom two, the ventricles, are where the blood is pumped out again (*ventriculus* is Latin for 'little belly'). Of all four chambers, it is the left ventricle that contracts most powerfully, which is why it is easiest to feel the heart pumping on the left side of the chest. The two sides of the heart are separated by a dividing wall called a septum; valves connect each atrium to the ventricle underneath it, allowing blood to flow forwards but never backwards; blood vessels carry the blood around.

How it works: Nerve signals from the brain produce electrical energy that stimulates the heart to contract (pushing blood into the chambers) and relax (pushing blood out of the chambers). These nerve signals tell the heart to speed up or slow down, according to how hard the body is working at that moment: whether it is sleeping, running for the bus, making love. It is one of the few muscles that works involuntarily, so that one doesn't have to think about it.

Number of beats (i.e. number of times it contracts and relaxes) per minute: between 70 and 80, which adds up to about 42 million beats a year.

Amount of blood pumped around the body by the heart: About 5.6 litres, which in a single day travels a total of 12,000 miles as it circulates around the body.

Amount of time a tap would have to be turned on to equal the amount of blood pumped by the heart in an average lifetime: Forty-five years.

The only cells in the body that do not receive blood: The cornea — that is, the transparent part of the eye that covers the eye and the pupil. Its need to be transparent means it has no blood vessels, but instead receives nutrients from tear fluid and aqueous humour. All the body's other 75 trillion cells have blood pumped to them.

The reason for the 'thump-thump' sound of a heartbeat: It is the sound of the four valves of the heart closing.

Origin of the term 'heart-felt': Aristotle believed that the source of human emotions was the sensory input that travelled from the peripheral organs via blood vessels to the heart.

The history of the stethoscope: It was invented by a French doctor named René Laënnec because he felt it was improper to place his ear against the chest of his female patients. He wrote:

> In 1816, I was consulted by a young woman presenting general symptoms of heart disease. Owing to her stoutness little information could be gathered by application of the hand and percussion. The patient's age and sex did not permit me to resort to direct application of the ear to the chest. I recalled a well-known acoustic phenomenon; namely, if you place your ear against one end of a wooden beam the scratch of a pin at the other extremity is distinctly audible. It occurred to me that this physical property might serve a useful purpose in the case with which I was then dealing. Taking a sheet of paper I rolled it into a very tight roll, one end of which I placed on the pericardial region, whilst I put my ear to the other. I was both surprised and gratified at being able to hear the beating of the heart with much greater clearness and distinctness than I had ever before by the direct application of my ear.

Origin of the iconography of the heart: Nobody really knows. It could be that it derives from a plant called silphium, found in the Greek city of Cyrene (in today's Libya), which has heart-shaped seedpods that were thought to have contraceptive properties. Silphium was so important to the city's economy that coins were issued depicting the seedpod, associating it with sex and then love. Others have suggested that Aristotle's inaccurate description of the heart as a three-chambered organ, round at the top and pointed at the bottom, resulted in the way it is typically drawn today.

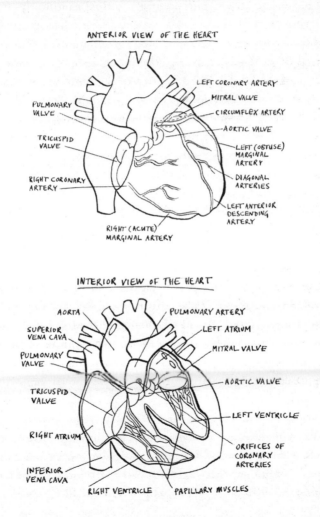

ANTERIOR VIEW OF THE HEART

LEFT CORONARY ARTERY
MITRAL VALVE
PULMONARY VALVE
CIRCUMFLEX ARTERY
AORTIC VALVE
TRICUSPID VALVE
LEFT (OBTUSE) MARGINAL ARTERY
DIAGONAL ARTERIES
RIGHT CORONARY ARTERY
LEFT ANTERIOR DESCENDING ARTERY
RIGHT (ACUTE) MARGINAL ARTERY

INTERIOR VIEW OF THE HEART

AORTA
PULMONARY ARTERY
SUPERIOR VENA CAVA
LEFT ATRIUM
PULMONARY VALVE
MITRAL VALVE
TRICUSPID VALVE
AORTIC VALVE
LEFT VENTRICLE
RIGHT ATRIUM
ORIFICES OF CORONARY ARTERIES
INFERIOR VENA CAVA
RIGHT VENTRICLE
PAPILLARY MUSCLES

RING-A-DING-DING

THE fourth finger, *digitus quartus, digitus medicinalis, digitus annularis*: this particular part of your anatomy is most commonly known as the 'ring' finger, for obvious reasons. Centuries ago, you were free to wear your engagement ring on whichever finger you felt like, though it was especially fashionable to have it adorn the thumb of the left hand: each joint in the hand was dedicated to a different saint, and this one belonged to the Virgin Mary. The reason it later became traditional to wear it on the fourth finger of the left hand is that the vein (*vena amoris*) that leads to it was thought to be directly connected to the heart.

ENGAGEMENT RING OPTIONS

While many of us have our engagement ring foisted upon us by our betrothed posing as a benevolent fashion dictator (no advice is offered here about what to do if the engagement ring is not up to scratch: 'tis a conundrum beyond the realms of etiquette, decided primarily by the temperament of the groom-to-be), others are presented with the less-romantic-but-more-practical option of choosing it jointly. What sort of ring to choose is actually one of the less trivial decisions you will make during these fraught few months: remember, you are stuck with it *forever*.

When deciding upon an engagement ring, ensure it does not feature a diamond mined in Angola, Sierra Leone or the Congo, which are the world's top three producers of conflict ('blood') diamonds. The proportion of the world's total diamond production that are conflict diamonds has fallen in recent years from a peak of 15 per cent in 1990 to only 1 per cent in 2012, but this does not mean it is not still a problem. As for settings, those like the Tiffany setting (invented in 1886) ought to be banned if only for safety reasons — gosh, they are lethal — though they are excellent for fending off muggers. Otherwise, there are a thousand other engagement ring options that any jeweller would be thrilled to discuss with you. Do also consider personalizing your ring in some way, for example by having your initials engraved on the inside. This at least ensures it is non-transferable . . .

STOCK PRICE ANALYSIS

The high street option: Signet Jewelers (owners of H. Samuel, Ernest Jones and Leslie Davis, and the No. 1 jewellery company in the UK)

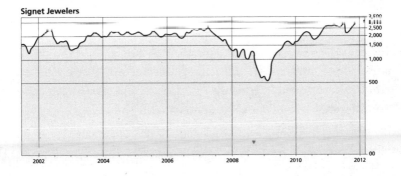

Price per share in pence on the London Stock Exchange from 2002 to 2012

The classic option: Harry Winston (as referenced by Marilyn Monroe in 'Diamonds Are a Girl's Best Friend')

Harry Winston Diamond Corporation

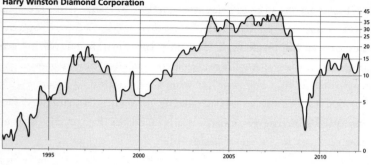

Price per share in cents on the New York Stock Exchange from 1993 to 2012

The naff-so-only-to-impress-your-friends option: Tiffany

Tiffany & Co.

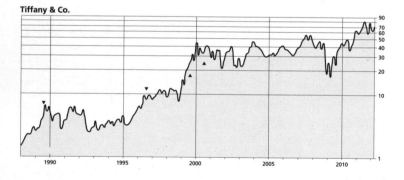

Price per share in cents on the New York Stock Exchange from 1988 to 2012

The thing is, if you have any taste at all, a vintage ring is the only way forward. The disadvantage is that a vintage ring usually has to be bought over the Internet if one is to get the best price, and this is a terrifying prospect. It is worth it, though, even if it does mean that one of the most expensive purchases you or your betrothed will ever make in your life gets packaged up and entrusted to the Royal Mail. Eek.

HOW TO CLEAN A DIAMOND RING

Wash the ring in warm water with mild soap once a week, then air dry it on some loo roll and polish it with a soft cloth. Once every couple of years, take to a jeweller for a steam or ultrasonic clean; also ask them to check that the diamond is still sitting securely in its setting. One does not want it to fall out during a frantic bout of dancing or a heated, arm-waving argument.

MOST PUBLISHED PASSAGE ABOUT LOVE AND MARRIAGE EVER (PART 1)

DID you know that it is actually illegal to publish a book about marriage without including Shakespeare's incredibly simple but ridiculously perfect Sonnet 116 (first published in 1609)? Well, OK, not illegal exactly, but it certainly should be. Quotations relating to love and marriage are almost always trite, clichéd, sexist or dull. There are only two that are not, and anyone who thinks otherwise is not only wrong but also quite possibly feeble-minded. One is below; another appears on page 180. Consider learning these off by heart, not only because everyone should know a few poems off by heart so that they have something to recite whilst giving birth or climbing Everest, but also because it is helpful during a marital row to recite to oneself whilst taking deep breaths.

> Let me not to the marriage of true minds
> Admit impediments. Love is not love
> Which alters when it alteration finds,
> Or bends with the remover to remove:
> O no! it is an ever-fixed mark
> That looks on tempests and is never shaken;
> It is the star to every wandering bark,
> Whose worth's unknown, although his height be taken.
> Love's not Time's fool, though rosy lips and cheeks
> Within his bending sickle's compass come:
> Love alters not with his brief hours and weeks,

But bears it out even to the edge of doom.
If this be error and upon me proved,
I never writ, nor no man ever loved.

Of course we've all heard this poem a hundred million times before, but it is worth re-reading it periodically in order to remember what it is to which we aspire. Aim high.

LET THE SUN SHINE IN

FOR those who choose to get married in the spring or summer, the weather becomes a matter of obsession in the weeks before a wedding; meanwhile, those geniuses who plump for a winter date sit back and bask smugly in the assumption that the weather will almost certainly be terrible (rain, snow, probably hail too just for fun) and thus they can efficiently plan around it. There are over two hundred automatic weather stations across the UK, collecting a range of detailed meteorological data at one-minute intervals which are then transmitted to the Met Office's central collection office in Exeter to be collated and analysed. Hopefully the information they offer can help the bride-to-be calm her nerves, whatever season she has chosen for her wedding.

MAP OF THE MAIN UK WEATHER STATIONS

HOURS OF SUNSHINE IN THE UK (1981–2010 WEATHER STATION AVERAGES)

		Jan.	Feb.	Mar.	Apr.	May	Jun.	Jul.	Aug.	Sept.	Oct.	Nov.	Dec.	Yearly Total
1	Bognor Regis	75.4	94.6	130.9	198.6	233.0	237.9	252.5	236.7	174.1	131.9	88.5	66.7	1920.8
2	Eastbourne	70.5	89.7	127.7	198.1	232.8	239.8	253.3	236.7	172.0	124.5	83.7	59.2	1887.9
3	Everton	65.9	86.3	124.2	186.3	221.7	225.8	233.0	221.3	162.1	118.9	79.7	56.4	1781.6
4	Teignmouth	64.7	83.5	122.6	186.3	217.5	222.4	225.0	209.6	160.6	110.6	84.0	60.4	1747.1
5	St Mawgan	66.6	86.4	125.0	194.2	220.5	216.1	207.7	202.6	164.1	117.2	79.2	63.2	1742.5
6	Boscombe Down	62.2	80.8	119.2	175.0	205.9	217.7	223.3	205.3	152.3	114.9	75.1	57.8	1689.4
7	Wattisham	63.9	83.0	116.0	173.7	211.9	208.5	217.3	204.5	151.7	119.8	74.8	56.6	1681.5
8	Tenby	62.7	83.4	119.5	185.3	215.6	209.8	209.9	197.7	150.7	107.9	69.9	54.2	1666.5
9	Valley	62.3	86.5	123.1	177.8	231.8	207.8	201.1	189.5	146.7	109.7	63.6	51.6	1651.4
10	Wye	59.6	79.6	115.3	174.1	205.2	200.1	213.7	210.3	152.2	118.2	71.9	49.8	1649.9
11	Bude	60.9	84.2	116.7	179.7	212.5	193.3	190.7	189.4	157.1	109.4	73.2	57.3	1624.3
12	Aberporth	63.1	83.0	120.0	177.6	217.4	206.4	199.1	184.1	146.8	105.6	64.4	53.2	1620.6
13	Lyneham	58.5	78.1	114.5	166.8	199.6	201.3	212.2	199.0	148.9	111.4	70.4	50.8	1611.3
14	Waddington	61.8	83.2	117.0	159.6	205.6	187.5	206.5	192.7	144.2	113.3	71.5	55.4	1598.3
15	Rothamsted	60.6	77.3	111.7	159.9	193.9	199.1	207.1	199.1	143.7	113.2	69.1	50.6	1585.3
16	Ronaldsway	54.1	77.9	115.9	171.2	227.6	203.4	197.4	184.9	138.9	103.6	63.5	46.0	1584.6
17	Oxford	62.5	78.9	111.2	160.9	192.9	191.0	207.0	196.5	141.2	111.3	70.7	53.8	1577.9
18	Ross-on-Wye	54.0	75.2	113.6	163.1	195.5	201.5	215.2	197.8	142.6	104.3	63.4	45.0	1571.2
19	Blackpool	56.0	78.9	112.3	168.6	217.9	201.2	197.8	182.9	141.9	98.8	61.9	48.1	1566.5

20	Leuchars	62.3	85.1	126.0	158.6	203.8	187.4	188.3	174.9	138.3	107.8	79.4	52.4	1564.3
21	Wisley	54.8	75.2	110.9	161.9	192.6	195.4	206.3	200.4	144.1	113.6	65.1	44.0	1564.2
22	Yeovilton	55.0	75.6	113.0	166.1	193.5	195.5	202.3	192.7	143.9	104.9	70.6	50.9	1563.8
23	Marham	56.8	78.7	104.5	161.1	203.8	189.5	206.7	191.8	137.7	111.2	68.7	49.6	1560.1
24	Bedford	63.6	83.1	106.8	168.2	201.4	183.4	197.6	187.2	138.5	109.3	66.0	54.3	1559.2
25	Lowestoft	51.7	78.0	114.1	174.8	202.4	181.0	196.4	199.8	147.0	111.0	62.4	40.8	1559.2
26	Cardiff	54.4	75.9	111.9	169.6	190.6	190.0	199.0	190.7	149.6	103.0	65.8	48.9	1549.4
27	Boulmer	64.2	83.3	123.3	157.4	198.7	188.0	182.7	173.4	138.5	107.8	75.1	54.6	1547.0
28	Cleethorpes	61.1	82.4	111.1	160.5	199.0	182.3	201.6	184.1	136.0	105.0	66.5	50.3	1539.8
29	Colwyn Bay	56.2	81.8	115.0	162.8	209.0	185.6	189.6	174.7	135.2	108.2	59.9	44.1	1522.0
30	Aspatria	47.5	77.0	114.0	159.8	217.1	195.2	191.6	179.8	136.1	98.7	61.2	41.6	1519.6
31	Cambridge	58.3	77.1	110.7	152.5	179.4	176.7	187.6	182.6	139.5	113.9	66.7	49.3	1494.5
32	High Mowthorpe	52.3	76.6	110.0	149.5	198.8	179.1	191.9	178.4	139.4	104.8	64.4	46.6	1491.7
33	Greenwich	49.9	71.4	107.1	159.8	181.2	181.0	192.1	195.1	138.9	108.1	58.5	37.4	1480.5
34	Tiree	39.0	69.9	111.1	175.2	238.8	205.5	174.4	163.3	128.2	88.4	46.8	36.0	1476.6
35	Shawbury	53.2	72.4	104.5	148.5	188.9	180.7	192.4	175.6	131.7	99.4	61.1	45.4	1453.7
36	Durham	58.6	80.3	115.5	150.3	181.7	164.8	172.3	167.3	134.5	102.8	66.4	51.2	1445.4
37	Sheffield	45.2	68.3	111.9	144.0	190.9	179.5	199.5	185.0	136.2	90.7	53.7	40.0	1444.9
38	Craibstone	60.6	84.9	120.3	151.5	194.1	163.8	159.3	160.4	124.6	100.0	65.4	47.7	1432.6
39	Sutton Bonnington	52.3	74.4	107.4	143.9	178.2	158.1	188.0	179.0	134.1	104.0	60.9	43.3	1423.5
40	Edinburgh	49.5	78.3	114.6	147.0	191.2	171.0	173.5	160.0	128.6	100.8	65.9	40.4	1420.7
41	Stratford-upon-Avon	52.3	68.1	101.9	143.1	177.1	171.1	189.6	179.2	131.8	101.3	58.6	44.9	1418.9
42	Trawscoed	45.5	69.7	89.1	159.8	191.0	178.4	176.6	180.6	132.3	96.8	57.8	39.5	1417.1
43	Manchester Airport	52.5	73.9	99.0	146.9	188.3	172.5	179.7	166.3	131.2	99.3	59.5	47.1	1416.2
44	Penkridge	47.9	65.5	97.5	139.6	179.6	164.2	183.6	168.1	124.9	97.8	57.3	38.3	1364.3
45	Aldergrove	49.7	71.2	102.5	153.3	197.7	167.9	151.3	142.1	119.9	91.2	59.4	46.2	1352.5
46	Auchincruive	44.0	68.8	98.0	140.0	198.0	160.0	158.6	151.6	111.6	98.0	80.1	38.3	1335.6
47	Kinloss	46.3	75.4	106.8	138.8	190.2	158.7	152.1	138.9	116.7	88.2	54.7	39.9	1306.8
48	Paisley	37.6	66.9	98.6	134.5	180.1	158.9	154.3	146.8	114.9	85.2	54.0	33.1	1265.0
49	Armagh	46.4	69.0	96.6	142.6	173.5	144.2	137.0	133.3	113.9	90.2	58.5	40.3	1245.5
50	Newton Rigg	38.8	59.0	97.0	135.4	166.9	161.7	160.1	145.5	114.6	79.4	41.7	37.2	1237.3
51	Stornoway	33.1	58.9	98.1	148.0	202.3	165.7	132.7	128.4	105.4	80.5	42.4	28.5	1223.8
52	Dunstaffnage	33.3	62.0	89.2	143.6	191.0	170.3	137.5	137.7	98.0	76.5	45.9	34.4	1219.4
53	Braemar	27.9	57.0	100.7	137.9	180.2	162.2	158.8	147.3	114.9	70.7	38.1	21.0	1216.4
54	Kinbrace	37.2	67.1	100.8	140.2	187.0	147.8	134.2	127.7	110.1	83.2	46.4	26.8	1208.6
55	Carmoney	26.6	62.1	89.2	142.7	181.5	141.1	126.2	124.9	100.6	81.1	47.2	39.3	1175.6
56	Eskdalemuir	38.0	61.2	86.4	128.3	168.5	143.7	147.8	135.7	103.1	73.1	49.8	38.8	1174.3
57	Kirkwall	32.2	59.3	98.2	136.8	190.0	148.6	132.2	129.7	105.3	75.8	40.1	24.5	1172.4
58	Ardtalnaig	21.3	56.1	92.9	133.0	173.2	155.8	152.0	141.3	104.2	67.9	33.3	11.8	1142.8
59	Malham Tarn	36.8	58.0	83.2	124.9	158.3	137.4	142.8	139.8	107.5	74.8	43.9	35.4	1142.7
60	Lerwick	27.2	55.2	94.1	131.8	181.0	146.2	124.4	127.9	101.3	68.8	33.8	18.1	1109.9
61	Kinlochewe	18.0	41.7	67.2	111.1	152.2	123.9	111.3	104.7	80.4	49.4	23.5	14.6	898.0

Source: Met Office

HOW TO WEAR WHITE

Louisa was married in the spring. Her wedding dress, of tulle frills and sprays of orange blossom, was short to the knee and had a train, as was the hideous fashion then. Jassy got very worked up about it.

'So unsuitable.'

'Why, Jassy?'

'To be buried in, I mean. Women are always buried in their wedding dresses, aren't they? Think of your poor old dead legs sticking out.'

'Oh, Jassy, don't be such a ghoul. I'll wrap them up in my train.'

'Not very nice for the undertakers.'

Nancy Mitford, The Pursuit of Love (1945)

SOME of us who shall remain nameless bought our wedding dress whilst out for a jog one Monday morning, having just happened to have stuffed a credit card inside our soon-to-be-sweaty sports bra just in case. At the time, this nameless person was living in a very hot country so chose the dress with this in mind, forgetting (ignoring?) the fact that her wedding was due to take place in England in mid-winter. The lesson? Don't take advice from her.

And yet . . . And yet. A few insights were gleaned from this debacle. The most important of them was this: never become so blasé about one's own wedding that one forgets to try. Do try, even just a bit. For whilst it is in every way desirable to resist turning into an obsessed bridezilla, it is at the same time polite to look as if one has made some effort. So look nice — maybe not the nicest you have ever looked or will ever look, and not ridiculously so, but just plain ole simple nice. All the rest is just detail, and as long as you look happy, only those who themselves recently got married will even notice.

And so to business. Cream puffs! Meringues! The Alps! Some brides-to-be secretly have a clear and long-held idea of the vision they wish to cut when they hoof it up that aisle, regardless of their feminist standpoint and steely persona. But fortunate is the bride who can genuinely get away with the dress she designed when she was eight years old, the sketch of which is stowed away in a box somewhere, alongside those Love Match calculations based on boys' names in her class. Which is where it should probably stay. For, although this star-spangled decision should be partially rooted in dreams, ideals and fantasy, some pressing practical concerns must also be heard, if one is not to look utterly bonkers.

There seems to be a perception that when it comes to choosing a wedding dress, the usual rules of fashion do not apply. This is a fallacy. They most certainly do; and should this need any re-inforcing, consider writing a note to this effect in thick black marker pen on your hand any time you approach a bridal shop or website, credit card in hand. So if you would not wear a strapless dress in 'real' life, why on earth would you for your wedding? Ditto the colour white, frankly: sorry to be a curmudgeon, but the truth is that it actually suits very few people.

BODY SHAPE

Before getting carried away with girly shopping dates – perhaps you are confused and mistakenly think you are a character in a Kate Hudson film? – you must work on attaining a realistic picture of your adult size and shape. Browse through current photographs to garner a sense of your proportions and the sort of dress shapes that might suit. If it is healthy and achievable to drop a dress size, work out a plan for cutting back on the cakes; or find out about classes at the local gym — there's nothing like a squealing loon in Lycra barking 'You, fatty at the back — get up off the floor!' to terrify the pounds from your reluctant bulk.

Pear-shaped: This is the most common body shape in the UK: small boobs, bigger bum. Go for slender-fitting A-line forms boasting square necklines, focusing your browsing particularly on strapless numbers. Flagging up a horizontal line at this level fools the beholder that they are studying a more balanced being. Aim to smooth out irrational proportions by drawing the eye as far from the hip as light angles and retinas allow. A-lines whisper over beefy hips, and conceal hefty thighs and lumpen botties, whilst showcasing a fabulously svelte torso.

Hourglass: You beast! This lady can wear *anything* and look fabulous (including the awe-inspiring fishtail!).

Size 18+: Scaffoldings of corsetry will do wonders for the tummy region, whilst longer lines and sheer accoutrements dotted about the place will blur edges as if in misty gossamer.

Short — sorry, 'petite': Heels heels heels — as high as can be borne. Or stilts. And a long skirt to cover the smoke-and-mirrors mess.

Throughout the process, remember that nobody ever remembers a meringue. What they remember is a vintage suit, or a blue silk jacket, or a fabulous hat, or gorgeous gloves. Go forth, be bold! The time is now.

SEASONAL CONCERNS

As we noted already when looking at weather patterns, winter weddings in the UK are easier to plan for in many respects, not least regarding dress choice. It *will* be cold. We know this. Which means that you do not have to worry about sweating, or bright colours clashing with your overheated countenance. You can plan for glamorous fur stoles, dashing velvet capes, fabulous little umbrellas, pashminas (if there is *really* no other option — ghastly!). Shoes will pinch less, as you will not have to worry about fleshy, heat-induced swelling. Bolder colours can generally be sported in the washed-out winter seasons, since the palette all around you is so diffuse and dismal, and the light so much gentler. You also have the very forgiving option of sleeves (though Ms Middleton obviously popularized the look for other seasons). Joy: you do not have to be concerned about bingo wings. Colourwise, go crazy! Thought about a festive scarlet, champagne gold, arctic blue or lashings of snowy-white fake fur? You clearly cannot get away with this stuff in the warmer months, yet it will be remembered fondly by your pallid and sun-starved winter guests for a long time to come.

COLOUR

The tastemakers all implore, beg and plead with you: do at least consider dress colours other than white. For centuries, women just got married in their 'best' dress, regardless of colour. It was only the Victorians' obsession with status that transformed a specially made white dress into a fashion statement, since it indicated that the bride was wealthy enough to be able to afford a dress she would only wear once. In other words, it was just a way to show off, yet this quickly morphed into the traditional white wedding that today is so ubiquitous.

Married in white, you have chosen all right;
Married in grey, you will go far away;
Married in black, you will wish yourself back;
Married in red, you wish yourself dead;
Married in green, ashamed to be seen;
Married in blue, he will always be true;
Married in pearl, you will live in a whirl;
Married in yellow, ashamed of your fellow;
Married in brown, you will live out of town;
Married in pink, your fortune will sink.

Traditional Victorian verse

For many, the point of wearing white is to make one appear to have luminous skin and hence to be eminently marriage-able. Engender the help of that brutally straight-talking pal to ascertain which shades one can genuinely get away with. To avoid looking like the Phantom Bride, steer clear of the purest whites, if your complexion more resembles a shocked snow-man than creamiest ivory. These days, anything goes, but do consider the venue, as well as the intended tone of the show, in order to measure the appropriateness of your desired hue. You do not wish to be ridiculed for your racy ruby or proud plum, or for your guests to feel that you are being worn *by* your garish choice. Equally, though, do not feel forced by tradition into something generically pallid. Splashes of a favourite colour in the form of a sash or shawl are often the preference of those not quite bold enough to be loud and proud about their dreamed-of colourscape. Also remember the words of the always-to-be-obeyed India Knight: the idea of wearing white over the age of thirty (these days one might perhaps nudge this up to thirty-five) is not to be entertained at all, ever, under any circumstances.

A TRAIN?

No, not to be waiting outside the reception in case you change your mind. Rather, that most fabulous of fashion statements that with one glance suggests to all onlookers that you have a stylist following you wherever you go to straighten and primp at every moment. Do it! This is (hopefully) your only shot at getting married, and there are likely to be few other circumstances where you would get to give wearing a train a go. And, if you are given to blushes or embarrassed grimaces, what better disguise as you haul yourself up the aisle, gawked at by so many? You can also arrange for a detachable one, so if you are feeling too bride-y later, just whip it off. With so many types of train to choose from, you can opt to go very understated with a 'duster', which does not drench the floor by more than about a foot. Or go crazy with a 'cathedral', which extends up to seven and a half feet from your waist. Easily damaged, but eminently stately.

SHOES

It is essential to wear comfortable shoes. This is not a euphemism.

TEN WEDDING DRESSES THAT CHANGED THE WORLD (OR AT LEAST DIVERTED THE WORLD'S ATTENTION FOR A DAY OR TWO UNTIL IT RETURNED TO WORRYING ABOUT MORE IMPORTANT THINGS, LIKE SHOES)

Jacqueline Kennedy (1953): Designed by Ann Lowe, a New York designer whose name, outrageously, did not appear in any newspaper accounts of the big day simply because she was African American. The dress she created for JK was full skirted and made with 50 yards of ivory silk taffeta, accessorized with a full veil and white gloves.

Audrey Hepburn (1954): Designed by Pierre Balmain. A full-skirted dress, which the bride wore with roses adorning her hair.

Grace Kelly (1956): Designed by Helen Rose, a costume designer for MGM. A long-sleeved, high-necked, very prim gown with a puffy skirt, fitted around a torso made of 25 yards of white silk taffeta, 100 yards of tulle, netting and *peau de soie* (a type of satin), and century-old rose point lace from Brussels. Kelly accessorized with a Juliet cap covered with orange blossom and seed pearls, a 90-yard-long tulle

veil and a bouquet of lilies of the valley.

Raquel Welch (1967): A crochet dress with a fur coat. The ultimate slutty bride. Good luck to her.

Yoko Ono (1969): A mini-dress with giant sunglasses and a giant sunhat. Archetypally 1960s.

Bianca Jagger (1971): Designed by Tommy Nutter, who may sound like a drummer in a band but was in fact a Savile Row tailor who almost single-handedly reinvented the concept of the Savile Row suit in the 1960s. For Jagger's wedding he created a white skirt-suit as well as a shirt to wear under the jacket but Jagger was four months pregnant at the time and the shirt did not fit. So instead, she just wore nothing at all underneath, to devastating effect.

Princess Diana (1981): Quite enough has been written about this dress in the past, thank you. There is no need for a single additional word here, except to say that it is probably the most famous wedding dress in history.

Brigitte Nielsen (1985): Nielsen designed it herself — clearly — but, for all its faults, it is the pre-eminent example of a 1980s wedding dress.

Kate Middleton (2011): Designed by Sarah Burton for Alexander McQueen, in case you have been living on Mars for the past couple of years.

Kate Moss (2011): Designed by John Galliano. A bias-cut, 1920s-style dress. For Kate to wear something ghastly to her own wedding would have augured Armageddon, so it was a huge relief when she turned up in the dreamiest dress ever. Isn't it wonderful when people live up to their own cliché?

ALL ABOUT THE NA PEOPLE OF CHINA; OR, IN PRAISE OF THE FURTIVE VISIT

IMAGINE a society without marriage. A society without husbands or fathers. The Na people of China are one of the very few societies in human history to live like this, and hence are a fascinating study in an alternative way to exist.

The Nas' main method of procreation is by means of a sexual practice unique to the tribe known as a 'furtive visit' (*nana sese*). This is a secret romantic encounter between a man and a woman, and thus almost the exact opposite to a formalized union such as a marriage: it is an entirely private affair, with no input whatsoever from either friends or family. Here's how it works.

A man or a woman can make the first move. One makes one's desire known through a specific, ritualized gesture that involves taking advantage of a moment when the chosen person is not paying attention and abruptly snatching away an object he or she is carrying. A smile in reaction signifies tacit agreement; firmly demanding the object's return suggests otherwise.

For a first-time furtive visit, the couple agree on a signal the man will use to gain access to the woman's bedroom: for example, a certain number of knocks on the window or a few lines of a certain song. Some visits are not planned in advance, in which case the man just persuades the woman on the spot; in this situation, it is advisable to bring along a pork bone or a pine cone full of rice to appease the guard dog that patrols almost every Na house at night-time. Usually the man arrives at about midnight, and leaves to return home at the first crow of the rooster. The intention is that no other members of the household are made aware of his presence. This also means that if a young man who has come to rob a house is surprised by a household member, he can easily protest his innocence by claiming he's simply there for a furtive visit. Sneaky.

A man makes visits either within his own village or in neighbouring villages. It is acceptable and even encouraged for him to pay two or three furtive visits a night. It is exceptionally rare for couples to make a vow of fidelity in the way they are encouraged to do in almost every other human society: for the Na, such a thing is seen as shameful, since it goes against their customs.

If a woman becomes pregnant as a result of a furtive visit, as of course often happens, the procedure is that

> At birth a child is automatically part of his or her mother's group. Those who have the same female ancestry all live together under one roof. In each generation the brothers and sisters work, eat and raise the children born to the sisters together. They live together their entire lives. Normally this kind of household can stay together for several generations without separating. The Na is therefore exclusively matrilineal.

This is according to Marco Polo, writing in the thirteenth century about his travels around China, and his account still holds up today. Among the Na, the husband/wife relationship is largely replaced by the brother/sister relationship. Brothers jointly provide for their sister's children, both materially and emotionally. Thus the uncle plays the role of father. None of the siblings bring an outsider of the opposite sex into the household as a permanent member; instead brothers and sisters live together as companions for life, with 'divorce' not an option. The oldest daughter and son within each family learn from the male and female chiefs of the older generation and gradually take over their position. The upshot is that the men of the household are not needed to procreate, but rather just to help parent and run the home.

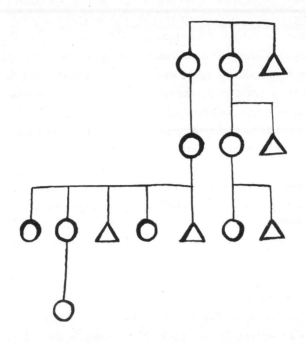

The Na people have existed in this way since before the Qing dynasty. Starting in 1986, there have been several attempts by the Chinese government to reform them and encourage marriage, but to no avail.

For more on all of this, plough your way through the utterly fascinating, albeit rather dense book *A Society without Fathers or Husbands: The Na of China* by the Chinese anthropologist Professor Cai Hua. Excellent if you are having trouble sleeping at night.

A BRIEF LEGAL HISTORY OF MARRIAGE; OR, MAKE SURE YOU KNOW WHAT YOU ARE GETTING YOURSELF INTO

Sixteenth-century London | It was illegal to beat one's wife *unless* it was after 9.00 p.m. and did not disturb the neighbours, in which case it was fine.

1753 | The Hardwicke Marriage Act was the earliest serious attempt to tighten up marriage law in England. It decreed that anyone under the age of twenty-one had to have parental consent. Also, for a wedding to be legal, the bride and groom had to obtain a licence and publish banns in advance, and the ceremony itself had to take place in a parish church or chapel and be conducted by a clergyman of the Church of England. Jews and Quakers were exempt, but Catholics, Muslims and people of every other religion had no option but to be married according to Anglican tradition; otherwise, the wedding was not legally recognized.

The result was an end to clandestine marriage in England, but an increase in clandestine marriage in Scotland, where the legislation did not apply – hence the sudden popularity of elopements to Gretna Green, which was just over the border. There were also more wife sales, whereby a husband took his wife to market day and sold her off at auction in a sort of mutually agreed method of divorce, as Thomas Hardy later described in *The Mayor of Casterbridge* (1886).

1836 | The Second Marriage Act allowed Christians who were not members of the Church of England to marry legally in their own churches. It also introduced the concept of civil marriages, which allowed Catholic ministers to act as registrars for the first time.

1857	The Matrimonial Causes Act allowed women to petition for divorce for the first time, rather than just men. The sole allowable grounds remained adultery, though.
1870	The First Married Women's Property Act let married women retain control of up to £200 of any money they earned after they were married. It also allowed them to inherit money or property without having to relinquish control of it to their husband.
1882	The Second Married Women's Property Act legally recognized a husband and a wife as two separate legal entities. This meant that women were able to sue and be sued, were responsible for paying and receiving their own damages and their own debts, and had a right to buy and sell their own stocks and shares.
1893	The Third Married Women's Property Act gave married women legal control of all property they owned at marriage and all property they earned or inherited after marriage. Progress indeed.
1929	The Age of Marriage Act raised the minimum age of marriage to sixteen for both sexes.
2004	The Civil Partnership Act allowed gay couples to get married.

There are strangely few readable books about the history of marriage, but if you do want to find out more, try Maureen Waller's recent *The English Marriage* (2009), which, though vague on the political and legal history, is full of fascinating personal stories of couples from the fifteenth century onwards. *For Better, For Worse: British Marriages, 1600 to the Present* by John Gillis (1985) is an idiosyncratic take on the subject and full of interesting anecdotes, but a bit dated. *Marriage, a History* by the American academic Stephanie Coontz (2005) takes a more general, international perspective.

WEDDING JUNKIES

THE date approaches. Feelings run high. Judgement is clouded. Bride, beware! Steelier ladies than you have, in this vulnerable state, committed the fatal error of elevating relationships that should stay firmly in the realm of 'colleague/ acquaintance' to that of actual *friendship*. Someone who offers a sympathetic word when one is exposed to the stomach-melting news that the Tiffany tiara is 'no longer available' or supplies a nugget of wisdom when one just can't settle the 'Drastically Dramatic' vs. 'Glitzy 'n' Ritzy' bouquet dispute. These near-strangers appear as Fairy Godmothers, like luminous beacons in hours dark and treacherous, and before long the newly acquired calligraphy pen that one attended an evening class to learn how to handle is puppet-mastering one's alabaster fingers into inscribing the letters of Fairy G's name on to an invitation! To your wedding! The event to which even some people you have known since schooldays have been declined entry!

Should we blame the bride alone for this trance-like tendency for maladaptive decision-making? Not necessarily. Lore has it that roaming among us is a breed adept at preying on the vulnerabilities of a lady in a delicate state, aware that she lives in terror of making mistakes she could potentially regret forever. These creatures lie in stealth, waiting for an opportunity to prove their worth to one's existence, only to disappear from one's life before the toner on one's honeymoon snaps has dried. Consider the following examples:

Who?	Pre-engagement relationship	Critical incident	Post-engagement relationship	To invite or not to invite?
Office receptionist	You'd nod hello and goodbye on the way to your desk. She put your calls through.	She was there when you got the call about the band not being available.	Buddy. She's sent you links to the 'hottest' local pub musicians within a 65-mile radius of your venue.	Get real. This is the *archetype*. Check this girl's diary: she'll disappear before the speeches to get to the motorway for her next Big Day.
Friend of a close friend	You've been enjoying her anecdotes at parties for years. She's a laugh, but the mutual contact is required to keep conversation flowing.	She sent a bottle of champagne when your engagement was announced.	Friend of a friend.	No. Send her a very sweet note, thanking her for her enormous kindness. Make no reference to the wedding. And don't promise to show her the photos as a sop. That's just cruel.
A kindred spirit at your new job	You've only known her for three weeks, but sensed a connection straight away. You can see this one sticking.	She bounced up on your first day, announcing that she owned the same scarf. She's clearly stylish — so for once, this is a good thing.	Comrade and confidante.	Do it. But tell her not to let on to the rest of the team. For career expediency, it wouldn't do to play favourites at this point.
Your cleaner	Well. She's your cleaner.	Tears sprang into her eyes when you showed her the ring.	She cries and shakes her head, as if in relieved disbelief, whenever you approach.	Great offence could be taken if you didn't. And she does have keys to your house . . .
An estranged pal	Though you haven't spoken since university, you still wonder about her, and whether this would be a good time to reintroduce her into your life.	Nothing — just this whimsical sense that your wedding could prove a healing event that heralds a union betwixt past 'n' present.	Can you be sure she's still alive?	Your need to tie up any straggly ends is pathological. There's a reason you no longer speak to this person. Drop it.

ALL ABOUT LE CREUSET

THE Brussels Fair, 1924. Two Belgian industrialists met, and fell in love — in a strictly business sense, of course. Octave Aubecq (area of expertise: enamelling) and Armand Desaegher (area of expertise: casting) both had a dream of establishing their own foundry which would specialize in saucepans coated in a porcelain enamel glaze. It took them less than a year to turn this dream into a reality, setting up their Le Creuset business in Fresnoy-le-Grand, a town about 120 miles north-east of Paris that was on the trade route for all the iron, coke and sand they required for the project. The first Le Creuset product was a cast-iron cocotte produced in the company's signature colour, 'flame', inspired by the look of molten cast iron when it gets very, very hot.

Le Creuset pots and pans are the best wedding present one can ask for. They literally last forever (as long as you don't do anything ridiculous like put them in the dishwasher), and even if you are not much of a cook they look eternally gorgeous, whether astride the stovetop or adorning the kitchen shelves. Aubergine is by far the chicest colour, and duck-egg blue is also great; orange — or rather, 'flame' — is classic, though it is a mystery who genuinely likes the colour orange. Sure, a single Le Creuset casserole pot might cost more than a wedding dress, but it is worth it. It is reason alone to embark upon married life; in some cases, the Le Creuset lasts longer than the marriage itself.

So be sure to put a complete set of Le Creuset at the very top of your wedding list. The most sensible place to have said list is of course John Lewis, and the most fabulous place Liberty's, also known as the Best Shop In The World. For most of us, however, there is no excuse not to ask for donations to charity instead. Not to is just being greedy.

THE figures below, showing the age and marital status of brides on marriage, offer a revealing glimpse through a window into people's lives in cold, hard, calculating numbers.

Year	Marital status	Number of brides	Age group						
			Under 16	16	17	18	19	Under 20	20–24
2010	Total	243,808	—	66	163	837	1,688	2,754	34,502
	Single	185,595	—	66	163	836	1,681	2,746	34,140
	Widowed	4,440	—	—	—	—	—	—	9
	Divorced	53,773	—	—	—	1	7	8	353
2009	Total	232,443	—	88	233	942	1,843	3,106	33,129
	Single	174,938	—	88	233	937	1,827	3,085	32,753
	Widowed	4,452	—	—	—	—	—	—	6
	Divorced	53,053	—	—	—	5	16	21	370
2005		247,805	—	126	308	1,420	2,510	4,364	38,003
	Single	176,505	—	126	307	1,416	2,498	4,347	37,416
	Widowed	5,385	—	—	—	—	—	—	10
	Divorced	65,915	—	—	1	4	12	17	577
2000		267,961	—	296	687	2,768	4,297	8,048	48,638
	Single	187,717	—	294	682	2,736	4,247	7,959	47,517
	Widowed	6,152	—	—	—	—	—	—	16
	Divorced	74,092	—	2	5	32	50	89	1,105
1995		283,012	—	427	985	3,429	5,416	10,257	73,212
	Single	198,603	—	427	984	3,405	5,353	10,169	70,981
	Widowed	7,540	—	—	—	—	—	—	40
	Divorced	76,869	—	—	1	24	63	88	2,191
1990		331,150	—	647	2,028	6,934	12,177	21,786	121,889
	Single	243,825	—	647	2,028	6,931	12,140	21,746	118,083
	Widowed	9,331	—	—	—	—	2	2	59
	Divorced	77,994	—	—	—	3	35	38	3,747

THE LAST 150 YEARS OR SO

It is the numerous anomalies that are so fascinating: the woman in her seventies who was getting married for the very first time (1855), the sixteen-year-old widow (1870), the two seventeen-year-old divorcees (1950).

25–29	30–34	35–39	40–44	45–49	50–54	55–59	60–69	70–79	80 and over
73,841	51,560	28,992	18,891	13,954	8,754	4,855	4,555	992	158
70,982	45,010	19,078	7,790	3,398	1,417	561	409	55	9
68	145	236	383	541	636	603	1,150	551	118
2,791	6,405	9,678	10,718	10,015	6,701	3,691	2,996	386	31
69,757	47,923	28,190	18,458	13,319	8,219	4,758	4,449	997	138
66,954	41,504	18,208	7,264	3,010	1,239	504	332	74	11
56	140	279	365	529	575	571	1,265	566	100
2,747	6,279	9,703	10,829	9,780	6,405	3,683	2,852	357	27
68,062	52,369	32,001	20,757	13,286	8,525	5,239	4,108	938	153
64,504	42,006	17,404	6,475	2,417	474	457	248	47	10
71	190	322	463	628	744	771	1,425	634	127
3,487	9,873	14,275	13,819	10,341	6,807	4,011	2,435	257	16
80,312	54,649	30,793	17,452	11,677	8,406	3,682	3,219	940	145
73,188	38,833	13,410	4,075	1,482	664	297	223	58	11
117	294	474	615	708	903	715	1,484	703	123
7,007	15,522	16,909	12,762	9,487	6,839	2,670	1,512	179	11
87,680	48,216	24,015	14,352	11,507	6,284	2,848	3,248	1,199	194
75,470	29,158	8,196	2,461	1,123	449	254	255	74	13
220	433	545	619	961	994	772	1,847	949	160
11,990	18,625	15,274	11,272	9,423	4,841	1,822	1,146	176	21
90,629	38,032	20,064	15,251	9,611	5,679	2,811	3,831	1,400	167
74,656	19,811	5,519	1,993	836	463	263	343	98	14
269	453	593	902	1,169	1,154	998	2,445	1,142	145
15,704	17,768	13,952	12,356	7,606	4,062	1,550	1,043	160	8

Year	Marital status	Number of brides	Age group						
			Under 16	16	17	18	19	Under 20	20–24
1985		346,389	–	1,867	4,840	13,892	21,328	41,927	149,174
	Single	258,089	–	1,867	4,839	13,882	21,272	41,860	142,941
	Widowed	11,269	–	–	–	1	2	3	118
	Divorced	77,031	–	–	1	9	54	64	6,115
1980		370,022	–	3,317	9,591	25,367	34,152	72,427	154,479
	Single	277,826	–	3,317	9,590	25,359	34,091	72,357	146,478
	Widowed	14,601	–	–	–	1	5	6	198
	Divorced	77,595	–	–	1	7	56	64	7,803
1975		380,620	–	5,262	14,354	34,371	40,624	94,611	151,781
	Single	298,217	–	5,261	14,353	34,363	40,568	94,545	144,630
	Widowed	17,748	–	1	–	3	10	14	251
	Divorced	64,655	–	–	1	5	46	52	6,900
1970		415,487	–	7,686	17,981	37,944	48,500	112,111	202,705
	Single	364,397	–	7,686	17,981	37,939	48,481	112,087	198,506
	Widowed	17,406	–	–	–	3	5	8	308
	Divorced	33,684	–	–	–	2	14	16	3,891
1965		371,127	–	6,469	17,312	36,186	44,032	103,999	174,091
	Single	331,713	–	6,468	17,311	36,181	44,006	103,966	171,766
	Widowed	15,842	–	1	1	3	14	19	262
	Divorced	23,572	–	–	–	2	12	14	2,063
1960		343,614	–	5,089	13,298	25,827	37,497	81,711	164,802
	Single	309,473	–	5,089	13,294	25,827	37,481	81,691	163,439
	Widowed	16,412	–	–	3	–	9	12	269
	Divorced	17,729	–	–	1	–	7	8	1,094
1955		357,918	–	2,346	8,811	21,234	34,771	67,162	170,960
	Single	318,754	–	2,346	8,810	21,233	34,754	67,143	169,668
	Widowed	18,271	–	–	–	1	7	8	221
	Divorced	20,893	–	–	1	–	10	11	1,071
1950		358,490	–	1,364	5,882	16,480	28,806	52,532	166,399
	Single	315,036	–	1,364	5,876	16,479	28,791	52,510	164,721
	Widowed	21,057	–	–	4	–	3	7	343
	Divorced	22,397	–	–	2	1	12	15	1,335

25–29	30–34	35–39	40–44	45–49	50–54	55–59	60–69	70–79	80 and over
70,495	30,055	20,079	12,217	8,439	5,110	2,858	4,258	1,606	171
52,654	12,753	4,233	1,471	756	526	339	387	155	14
371	511	818	1,023	1,325	1,395	1,237	3,005	1,316	147
17,470	16,791	15,028	9,723	6,358	3,189	1,282	866	135	10
58,767	31,259	16,997	11,261	8,052	5,657	3,874	5,475	1,650	124
39,655	11,370	3,449	1,565	996	743	517	532	152	12
455	759	936	1,217	1,658	1,949	1,940	4,029	1,350	104
18,657	19,130	12,612	8,479	5,398	2,965	1,417	914	148	8
57,715	23,923	14,002	9,879	8,449	7,043	4,376	6,967	1,742	132
39,444	9,458	3,573	2,022	1,523	1,176	734	899	192	21
654	802	984	1,416	2,286	2,732	2,185	4,901	1,416	107
17,617	13,663	9,445	6,441	4,640	3,135	1,457	1,167	134	4
44,594	16,104	9,373	7,170	6,923	5,154	3,941	5,894	1,424	94
34,911	8,371	3,674	2,230	1,679	1,056	776	912	183	12
614	766	1,039	1,542	2,515	2,543	2,383	4,429	1,180	79
9,069	6,967	4,660	3,398	2,729	1,555	782	553	61	3
39,231	15,084	9,743	7,915	6,156	5,143	3,562	5,019	1,107	77
33,033	9,608	4,978	3,093	1,839	1,383	908	940	192	7
568	759	1,109	1,789	2,561	2,448	1,996	3,881	881	69
5,630	4,717	3,656	3,033	2,056	1,312	658	398	34	1
40,291	16,637	10,980	7,420	6,847	5,134	3,596	4,454	999	51
36,290	12,228	6,130	3,150	2,424	1,665	984	879	127	5
611	852	1,433	1,797	2,509	2,403	2,107	3,303	855	46
3,390	3,557	3,417	2,473	1,914	1,066	505	272	17	–
52,224	23,036	12,585	9,600	7,637	5,506	3,486	3,875	861	45
47,366	16,309	6,822	4,190	2,990	1,842	937	734	125	7
795	1,539	1,948	2,339	2,653	2,660	2,120	2,924	720	38
4,063	5,188	3,815	3,071	1,994	1,004	429	217	16	–
66,596	25,546	16,382	10,414	7,402	4,868	3,100	3,306	700	36
58,743	17,426	9,081	5,100	3,182	1,681	893	703	96	8
1,880	2,646	2,983	2,654	2,718	2,496	1,948	2,466	591	27
5,973	5,474	4,318	2,660	1,502	691	259	137	13	1

Year	Marital status	Number of brides	Under 16	16	17	18	19	Under 20	20-24
1945		397,626	–	1,582	6,487	18,007	30,923	56,999	194,022
	Single	363,549	–	1,582	6,487	17,993	30,878	56,940	191,169
	Widowed	26,065	–	–	–	13	43	56	2,549
	Divorced	8,012	–	–	–	1	2	3	304
1940		470,549	–	1,346	5,862	18,818	37,235	63,261	215,975
	Single	447,220	–	1,346	5,862	18,818	37,223	63,249	215,600
	Widowed	18,385	–	–	–	–	11	11	286
	Divorced	4,944	–	–	–	–	1	1	89
1935		349,536	–	814	2,988	8,750	16,164	28,716	157,738
	Single	331,751	–	814	2,988	8,750	16,163	28,715	157,397
	Widowed	15,179	–	–	–	–	–	–	279
	Divorced	2,606	–	–	–	–	1	1	65
1930		315,109	–	699	3,189	8,912	15,111	27,911	143,206
	Single	296,914	–	699	3,189	8,912	15,108	27,908	142,926
	Widowed	16,194	–	–	–	–	2	2	221
	Divorced	2,001	–	–	–	–	1	1	59
1925		295,689	26	276	1,885	6,991	13,449	22,627	134,198
	Single	275,756	26	276	1,885	6,991	13,445	22,623	133,844
	Widowed	18,574	–	–	–	–	3	3	314
	Divorced	1,359	–	–	–	–	1	1	40
1920		379,982	34	256	1,801	8,344	17,547	27,982	167,226
	Single	338,697	34	256	1,801	8,343	15,537	27,971	164,735
	Widowed	40,229	–	–	–	1	10	11	2,421
	Divorced	1,056	–	–	–	–	–	–	70
1915		360,885	21	186	1,443	7,216	15,049	23,915	160,774
	Single	336,724	21	186	1,441	7,216	15,047	23,911	160,213
	Widowed	23,743	–	–	2	–	2	4	550
	Divorced	418	–	–	–	–	–	–	11
1910		267,721	18	137	997	5,247	11,363	17,762	121,240
	Single	250,816	18	137	997	5,247	11,359	17,758	120,869
	Widowed	16,567	–	–	–	–	4	4	371
	Divorced	338	..	..	..	..	..	..	..

25–29	30–34	35–39	40–44	45–49	50–54	55–59	60–69	70–79	80 and over
71,925	28,971	15,621	9,994	6,788	4,361	2,806	2,930	508	17
66,211	23,424	11,115	5,872	3,239	1,724	920	654	69	3
4,270	3,459	2,727	2,849	2,937	2,312	1,773	2,215	437	14
1,444	2,088	1,779	1,273	612	325	113	61	2	—
109,584	37,504	16,988	9,408	6,076	3,870	2,297	2,711	471	17
107,507	34,095	13,132	5,685	2,940	1,531	765	628	69	4
1,217	2,092	2,661	2,957	2,744	2,135	1,471	2,039	398	13
860	1,317	1,195	766	392	204	61	44	4	—
98,902	30,918	12,419	6,914	4,585	2,980	1,857	2,084	400	15
97,327	28,202	9,438	4,189	2,319	1,229	632	569	59	2
1,063	1,911	2,391	2,385	2,107	1,667	1,203	1,500	340	13
512	805	590	340	159	84	22	15	1	—
85,522	26,116	11,791	6,740	4,638	3,017	1,924	1,951	392	12
83,926	23,299	8,596	3,954	2,226	1,227	684	559	54	—
1,184	2,223	2,747	2,532	2,280	1,717	1,231	1,385	338	12
412	594	448	254	132	73	9	7	—	—
79,596	27,043	12,229	6,731	4,516	2,899	1,717	1,686	276	13
77,909	23,476	8,749	3,748	2,111	1,010	502	414	29	1
1,661	3,161	3,339	2,825	2,333	1,823	1,205	1,265	237	12
275	406	341	164	72	36	10	7	—	—
102,694	38,465	17,892	9,416	5,930	3,313	1,996	1,735	253	10
93,542	29,242	11,300	4,899	2,573	1,153	514	313	25	—
8,878	8,926	6,383	4,398	3,303	2,136	1,479	1,420	228	10
274	297	209	119	54	24	3	2	—	—
100,395	39,044	16,765	9,186	5,696	3,010	1,408	1,265	706	6
97,974	31,797	12,061	4,797	2,347	969	381	189	22	2
2,333	3,925	4,594	4,263	3,258	2,063	1,115	1,075	183	4
88	122	114	46	21	8	2	1	—	—
75,091	25,922	11,251	5,779	3,771	2,078	1,145	893	138	4
73,400	23,023	8,039	3,176	1,588	647	266	148	23	2
1,691	2,899	3,212	2,603	2,183	1,431	879	745	115	2
..	..	..	..	..	..	..	..	..	..

Year	Marital status	Number of brides	Under 16	16	17	18	19	Under 20	20–24
1905		260,742	10	126	1,012	5,401	12,472	19,021	124,580
	Single	243,995	10	126	1,012	5,401	12,468	19,017	124,143
	Widowed	16,482	–	–	–	–	4	4	437
	Divorced	265	..	..	..	..	..	..	..
1900		257,480	17	140	1,040	6,061	13,825	21,083	125,196
	Single	239,774	17	140	1,040	6,059	13,822	21,078	124,741
	Widowed	17,518	–	–	–	2	3	5	455
	Divorced	188	..	..	..	..	..	..	..
	Widowed	13,875	–	1	–	1	3	5	319
	Divorced	..	..	..	..	..	..	..	..
1895		228,204	15	128	1,175	5,949	13,076	20,343	110,436
	Single	210,808	15	128	1,175	5,949	13,069	20,336	109,956
	Widowed	17,265	–	–	–	–	7	7	480
	Divorced	131	..	..	..	..	..	..	..
1890		223,028	16	166	1,501	7,009	14,609	23,301	107,146
	Single	204,886	16	166	1,500	7,009	14,604	23,295	106,605
	Widowed	18,048	–	–	1	–	5	6	541
	Divorced	94	..	..	..	..	..	..	..
1885		197,745	20	217	1,782	7,395	13,385	22,799	90,417
	Single	180,244	20	217	1,782	7,394	13,377	22,790	89,844
	Widowed	17,423	–	–	–	1	8	9	573
	Divorced	78	..	..	..	..	..	..	..
1880		191,965	28	272	1,707	6,782	12,326	21,115	79,782
	Single	173,695	28	272	1,707	6,781	12,319	21,107	79,183
	Widowed	18,213	–	–	–	1	7	8	599
	Divorced	57	..	..	..	..	..	..	..
1875		201,212	18	315	1,828	7,227	13,346	22,734	75,168
	Single	180,706	18	315	1,828	7,226	13,338	22,725	74,445
	Widowed	20,474	–	–	–	1	8	9	723
	Divorced	32	..	..	..	..	..	..	..
1870		181,655	36	289	1,602	5,967	11,033	18,927	61,572
	Single	164,200	36	288	1,602	5,967	11,020	18,913	60,959
	Widowed	17,441	–	1	–	–	13	14	613
	Divorced	14	..	..	..	..	..	..	..

25–29	30–34	35–39	40–44	45–49	50–54	55–59	60–69	70–79	80 and over
68,890	22,896	9,945	2,310	3,373	1,809	979	754	85	—
66,950	19,925	6,788	2,684	1,363	515	205	98	7	—
1,940	2,971	3,157	2,626	2,010	1,294	774	656	78	—
..	..	..	..	..	..	..	..	..	..
63,792	21,030	9,918	5,448	3,584	1,907	1,084	842	59	2
61,816	17,977	6,593	2,636	1,300	542	204	115	9	2
1,976	3,053	3,325	2,812	2,284	1,365	880	727	50	—
..	..	..	..	..	..	..	..	..	..
800	1,147	948	800	550	341	184	100	10	2
..	..	..	..	..	..	..	..	..	..
53,650	18,086	8,403	5,056	3,067	1,803	1,034	706	74	—
51,678	15,120	5,359	2,305	1,055	450	206	83	12	—
1,972	2,966	3,044	2,751	2,012	1,353	828	623	62	—
..	..	..	..	..	..	..	..	..	..
48,728	16,346	8,051	4,791	3,330	1,877	1,039	798	71	2
46,595	13,348	4,930	2,122	1,102	469	184	90	8	—
2,133	2,998	3,121	2,669	2,228	1,408	855	708	63	2
..	..	..	..	..	..	..	..	..	..
38,236	13,002	6,596	1,388	2,860	1,533	996	665	58	1
36,132	10,256	3,859	1,907	953	393	174	71	11	—
2,104	2,746	2,737	2,481	1,916	1,140	762	594	47	1
..	..	..	..	..	..	..	..	..	..
30,484	10,662	5,920	3,784	2,493	1,403	799	544	48	—
28,380	8,209	3,417	1,580	792	345	150	51	7	—
2,104	2,453	2,503	2,204	1,701	1,058	649	493	41	—
..	..	..	..	..	..	..	..	..	..
28,877	10,975	6,238	4,002	2,447	1,526	811	607	44	—
26,665	8,235	3,519	1,686	794	358	121	54	5	—
2,212	2,740	2,719	2,316	1,653	1,168	690	553	39	—
..	..	..	..	..	..	..	..	..	..
24,916	9,371	4,851	3,205	2,013	1,184	549	402	35	1
23,048	7,129	2,811	1,465	713	300	113	44	1	—
1,868	2,242	2,040	1,740	1,300	884	436	358	34	1
..	..	..	..	..	..	..	..	..	..

Year	Marital status	Number of brides	Age group						
			Under 16	16	17	18	19	Under 20	20–24
1865		185,474	41	262	1,526	5,212	9,724	16,765	59,382
	Single	168,311	41	262	1,525	5,210	9,716	16,754	58,856
	Widowed	17,142	–	–	1	2	8	11	526
	Divorced	21	..	..	..	..	..	..	..
1860		170,156	18	216	1,167	4,278	8,263	13,942	52,836
	Single	154,795	18	216	1,166	4,276	8,259	13,935	52,363
	Widowed	15,358	–	–	1	2	4	7	473
	Divorced	3	..	..	..	..	..	..	..
1855		152,113	32	202	833	3,229	6,280	10,576	43,135
	Single	137,678	32	202	832	3,228	6,273	10,567	42,706
	Widowed	14,435	–	–	1	1	7	9	429
	Divorced	..	..	..	..	..	..	..	..
1850		152,744	..	..	..	..	..	..	..
	Single	138,589	..	..	..	..	..	..	..
	Widowed	14,155	..	..	..	..	..	..	..
	Divorced	..	..	..	..	..	..	..	..

25–29	30–34	35–39	40–44	45–49	50–54	55–59	60–69	70–79	80 and over
23,525	8,796	4,730	3,208	1,935	1,072	516	401	40	2
21,914	6,763	2,841	1,446	713	270	92	43	4	1
1,611	2,033	1,889	1,762	1,222	802	424	358	36	1
..	..	..	..	..	..	..	..	..	..
20,815	8,093	4,357	2,894	1,675	938	478	324	29	1
19,403	6,333	2,690	1,384	588	239	78	30	1	—
1,412	1,760	1,667	1,510	1,087	699	400	294	28	1
..	..	..	..	..	..	..	..	..	..
17,650	7,317	3,762	2,427	1,380	817	366	250	15	1
16,377	5,722	2,352	1,128	478	223	62	30	1	—
1,273	1,595	1,410	1,299	902	594	304	220	14	1
..	..	..	..	..	..	..	..	..	..
..	..	..	..	..	..	..	..	..	..
..	..	..	..	..	..	..	..	..	..
..	..	..	..	..	..	..	..	..	..
..	..	..	..	..	..	..	..	..	..

Source: Office for National Statistics

THE EIGHT HUSBANDS OF ELIZABETH TAYLOR

MAY we humbly suggest that, when introducing your other half to new acquaintances, you use the term 'my current husband'? It hedges your bets most fabulously, and yes, it's funny *every* time and anyone who thinks otherwise clearly has no sense of humour. Lots of people really have had lots of husbands, but Elizabeth Taylor was the first high-profile serial wife. These days it seems rather eccentric to spend one's life in such a constant merry-go-round of marriage–divorce–marriage–divorce. And it is hard to fathom how one can change one's mind about a man's loveable qualities, or rather lack of, quite so rapidly as ET sometimes did, but then we are not the most famous woman on the planet (or are we? Hello, Madonna, welcome to these humble literary endeavours, glad to have you). But celebrity marriage is apparently a whole different world, where it never occurs to anyone to say, 'Let's just leave it six months and then reassess' or 'Let's try a bit harder and go to couples therapy'; instead, it's always, 'That's it, it's all over, I'm off to sleep with Rhys Ifans.' Anyway, whatever the circumstances, let us relive these well-known failed marriages: ET was reviled for many of them, but goodness, at least she did not chop off the heads of any of those she unlovingly discarded, unlike other serial marriers one could mention.

Date	Intended	Wedding details
6 May 1950–29 January 1951 (divorced)	Conrad 'Nicky' Hilton	Over six hundred guests at the Church of Good Shepherd in Beverly Hills followed by a reception at Bel Air Country Club. Dress was a big meringue with a tiara and 10 yards of veil. The entire day was stage-managed by MGM.
21 February 1952–26 January 1957 (divorced)	Michael Wilding	A fifteen-minute ceremony, with ET dressed in a grey wool suit, in Caxton Hall in London. Followed by a reception at Wilding's flat at 2 Bruton Street.
2 February 1957–22 March 1958 (Todd was killed in a plane crash; this was the only one of Taylor's marriages not to end in divorce)	Michael Todd	ET wore a blue cocktail dress for a ceremony at the hillside villa of former Mexican president Miguel Alemán in Acapulco in Mexico, followed by an outdoor reception with fireworks.
12 May 1959–6 March 1964 (divorced)	Eddie Fisher	The wedding venue was Temple Beth Shalom in Las Vegas (the vows were recited in English and in Hebrew). The ceremony was followed by a reception at the Hidden Well Ranch just outside the city. The bride wore a green chiffon dress with a high neckline, long sleeves and a loosely draped hood.

Date	Intended	Wedding details
15 March 1964–26 June 1974 (divorced)	Richard Burton	ET married the great love of her life in a suite at the Ritz-Carlton in Montreal in front of just eleven guests, almost all of whom were employees of either the bride or the groom. The service was a Unitarian one. ET was dressed in a replica of the yellow dress she wore in the first scene she shot with Burton in *Cleopatra*, and her hair decorated with white hyacinths.
10 October 1975–1 August 1976 (divorced)	Richard Burton (again)	This wedding took place next to a riverbank in Botswana in the Chobe Game Reserve. A district commissioner from the Tswana tribe officiated. ET wore a floor-length green gown decorated with brightly coloured birds.
4 December 1976–7 November 1982 (divorced)	John Warner	The couple married on Warner's ranch in the Virginia countryside amidst lots of cow pats left by Warner's prized herd of Hereford cattle. It was an Episcopal ceremony. The bride wore a lavender-grey dress with a lavender turban, grey suede boots and a fox fur coat, and carried a bouquet of heather.
6 October 1991–31 October 1996 (divorced)	Larry Fortensky	The venue this time was Michael Jackson's ranch, Neverland (Jackson also paid). There were 160 guests and the ceremony was conducted by a New Age guru, or 'spiritual psychotherapist' as she described herself. The outfit? A golden yellow dress designed by Valentino, with yellow roses in her hair.

Taylor herself said, 'I was taught by my parents that if you fall in love, if you want to have a love affair, you get married. I guess I'm very old-fashioned.' It clearly took her a long time to realize that she did not have to get married to get some lovin' in the bedroom. A revelation indeed.

WHITE

White . . . is not a mere absence of colour; it is a shining and
affirmative thing, as fierce as red, as definite as black . . . God
paints in many colours; but He never paints so gorgeously, I had
almost said so gaudily, as when He paints in white.

G. K. Chesterton

WHITE, ACCORDING TO THE OXFORD ENGLISH DICTIONARY

Etymology: Old English *hwít* = Old Frisian, Old Saxon *hwît*, Old
High German *(h)wî* (Middle High German *wî*, German *weiss*), Old
Norse *hvítr* (Swedish *vit*, Danish *hvid*), Gothic *hweits* < Old Germanic
*χwītaz. The grade χwit- is represented by Old Frisian *hwitt*
(Middle) Dutch, (Middle) Low German *wit* (-*tt*-) < *χwittaz,
probably < Indo-European *kwidnos, *kwitnos, the root of which is
found also in Sanskrit *çvid (perfect çiçvinde) to be white, Lithuanian
szvidùs bright, Latvian *svīst* to dawn, and Sanskrit *çvit* to be bright
or white, *çvitrá-* whitish, white, Avestan *spaeta* white, Lithuanian
szvintù to be bright, Old Church Slavonic *světŭ* light, *svitati* to
dawn . . .

[Definition] 1. a. Of the colour of snow or milk; having that
colour produced by reflection, transmission, or emission of all
kinds of light in the proportion in which they exist in the complete
visible spectrum, without sensible absorption, being thus fully
luminous and devoid of any distinctive hue.

c950   *Lindisf. Gosp.* John xx. 12 Tuoege engles in huitum gegerelum.

c1000   *West Saxon Gospels: Matt.* (Corpus Cambr.) v. 36 þu ne miht ænne locc gedon hwitne oððe blacne.

c1200   *Trin. Coll. Hom.* 57 Sume bereð clene cloð to watere to blechen him, Þat hit beo wit.

c1200   *Trin. Coll. Hom.* 163 Hire chemise is smal and hwit.

1297   *R. Gloucester's Chron.* (Rolls) 2786 Tueye grete dragons. Þe on was red þe oþer wyt.

a1300   *Cursor Mundi* 17288 + 216 Two aungels. Cled in white clothez.

c1300   *Havelok* (Laud) (1868) 1144 An hold with couel.

a1325   (1250) *Gen. & Exod.* (1968) l. 2810 In hise bosum he dede his hond: Quit and al unfer he it fond.

1340–70   *Alex. & Dind.* 719 A swan swiþe whit.

c1380   Wyclif *Wks.* (1880) 357 Þe oost sacrid, whijt & round.

c1400   (1380) *Pearl* (Nero) l. 220 Bornyste quyte was hyr uesture.

1423   *Kingis Quair* xlvi, Hir goldin haire and rich atyre couchit were with perllis quhite.

?1473   Caxton tr. R. Le Fèvre *Recuyell Hist. Troye* (1894) II. Epil. lf. 350, Myn eyen [are] dimmed with ouermoche lokyng on the whit paper.

1514   in H. Littlehales *Medieval Rec. London City Church* (1905) 20 Oon hole sute of vestymenttes, Whight or Blake.

1541   in J. W. Clay *Testamenta Eboracensia* (1902) VI. 135 A gowne the one side blake and the other side whitt.

1556   J. Heywood *Spider & Flie* lx. 5 With wheat tuskes fo[r]mde like a bore.

a1586   A. Montgomerie *Misc. Poems* xxv. 1 The tender snow, of granis soft & quhyt [*rhyme* delyte].

1590   Spenser *Faerie Queene* ii. iii. sig. P2, She Was yclad All in a silken Camus lylly whight.

a1650   E. Norgate *Miniatura* (1919) 52 Instead of abortive parchment, by some called Gilding Vellum, make use of your pure white velim.

1733   E. Budgell *Bee* II. 924 It proving a Maiden Assizes, the Sheriffs, according to Custom, presented the Judges with white Gloves.

1806   Scott *Palmer* i, The glen is white with the drifted snow.

1832   Tennyson *Miller's Daughter* xvii, in *Poems* (new ed.) 41 The lanes were white with May.

1860   J. Tyndall *Glaciers of Alps* ii. i. 227 White light is made up of an infinite number of coloured rays.

1912   C. N. Williamson & A. M. Williamson *Guests of Hercules* xvii, A round white moon that flooded the night with silver.

SHADES OF WHITE, ACCORDING TO MASTER COLOURISTS FARROW & BALL

All White: Farrow & Ball's cleanest and whitest white. It will bring a freshness to any colour.

Wimborne White: Named after the historic Dorset town in which John Farrow & Richard Ball founded Farrow & Ball.

Pointing: Named after the colour of lime pointing used in traditional brickwork.

James White: A soothing but fresh off-white with underlying green.

Clunch: As in the chalk building blocks used in East Anglia. A very versatile off-white.

Great White: A bright white but one that is neither 'yellow' nor 'cold'.

White Tie: The white of old, pre-brightened, starched cotton.

New White: Lighter and warmer than the much used Off-White. An ideal 'white' for use with some of the brighter colours.

House White: A light yellowed off-white.

Matchstick: Mostly used as a warm wall colour with lighter, cooler woodwork and ceiling whites.

String: A pale earth pigment-based colour that can be used either as an off-white with brighter colours or as its own colour with a brighter white.

Slipper Satin: A very successful off-white for woodwork with strong colours or as a wall colour used with many of the other whites, both lighter and darker.

Lime White: The colour of untinted brightest white limewash or soft distemper.

Off-White: Paler than Old White™ with which it could be used as a picking-out colour.

Cream: A classic colour based only on the addition of yellow ochre and in this case a little lamp black.

Dimity: Most used as a wall colour in its own right with All White or Pointing on woodwork and ceilings.

Joa's White: For devotees of Off-White, this colour, though just darker, has none the coolness or perceived greenish nature of Off-White.

Strong White: A bright, clean white when used with dark colours. Or if used with light colours it becomes cool.

Blackened: Historically made with the addition of 'lamp black', a pigment made by collecting the residue from burnt lamp oil.

Cornforth White: In memory of John Cornforth, architectural historian and author of the landmark publication *English Decoration in the 18th Century*.

Shaded White: Just darker than Off-White and lighter than Old White. This can also be used as a light 'drab' colour.

Hardwick White: The colourway used to touch up old white lime-wash at Hardwick Hall. Probably not thought of as white except in large areas or with strong dark colours.

Fawn: An often-used colour in eighteenth- and nineteenth-century decorating for both walls and woodwork.

Old White: This colour will look white in almost any 'old' situation.

Skimming Stone: A highly versatile off-white, 'Skimming' refers to its original use as a nineteenth-century skim colour.

(GET) INTO THE GROOVE

A hen night can take many forms, but all the best ones involve dancing, and ideally dancing to Madonna. For many of us, our relationship with Madonna resembles that with our first boyfriend. You fell in love aged twelve and have never really got over her; no matter what she does, no matter what crimes of taste or fashion or behaviour she is accused of, you just stick your fingers in your ears and sing 'la la laaaa' loudly and tunelessly until the chatter dies down. You alone understand that all she needs to do is realize she should be your best friend, and all her problems would be solved. So here, for your perusal, is a complete list of every song ever to have appeared on a Madonna album, so that you (or your maid or matron of honour) can plan the sound-track to your hen night in detail. Doesn't just reading it make you want to dig out all your tapes from the depths of your mum's attic?

Madonna (1983)

	Title	Writer	Producer	Length
1	'Lucky Star'	Madonna	Reggie Lucas, remix: John (Jellybean) Benitez	5 minutes 37 seconds
2	'Borderline'	Reggie Lucas	Reggie Lucas	5 minutes 20 seconds
3	'Burning Up'	Madonna	Reggie Lucas, remix: John (Jellybean) Benitez	3 minutes 45 seconds
4	'I Know It'	Madonna	Reggie Lucas	3 minutes 47 seconds
5	'Holiday'	Curtis Hudson, Lisa Stevens	John (Jellybean) Benitez	6 minutes 10 seconds
6	'Think of Me'	Madonna	Reggie Lucas	4 minutes 54 seconds
7	'Physical Attraction'	Reggie Lucas	Reggie Lucas, remix: John (Jellybean) Benitez	6 minutes 39 seconds
8	'Everybody'	Madonna	Mark Kamins	4 minutes 57 seconds

Like a Virgin (1984)

	Title	Writer	Producer	Length
1	'Material Girl'	Peter Brown, Robert Rans	Nile Rodgers	4 minutes 0 seconds
2	'Angel'	Madonna, Stephen Bray	Nile Rodgers	3 minutes 56 seconds
3	'Like a Virgin'	Tom Kelly, Billy Steinberg	Nile Rodgers	3 minutes 38 seconds
4	'Over and Over'	Madonna, Stephen Bray	Nile Rodgers	4 minutes 12 seconds
5	'Love Don't Live Here Anymore'	Miles Gregory	Nile Rodgers	4 minutes 47 seconds
6	'Dress You Up'	Andrea LaRusso, Peggy Stanziale	Nile Rodgers	4 minutes 1 second
7	'Shoo-Bee-Doo'	Madonna	Nile Rodgers	5 minutes 16 seconds
8	'Pretender'	Madonna, Stephen Bray	Nile Rodgers	4 minutes 30 seconds
9	'Stay'	Madonna, Stephen Bray	Nile Rodgers	4 minutes 7 seconds

True Blue (1986)

	Title	Writer	Producer	Length
1	'Papa Don't Preach'	Brian Elliot, Madonna	Madonna, Stephen Bray	4 minutes 48 seconds
2	'Open Your Heart'	Madonna, Gardner Cole, Peter Rafelson	Madonna, Patrick Leonard	4 minutes 13 seconds
3	'White Heat'	Madonna, Patrick Leonard	Madonna, Patrick Leonard	4 minutes 40 seconds
4	'Live to Tell'	Madonna, Patrick Leonard	Madonna, Patrick Leonard	5 minutes 52 seconds
5	'Where's the Party'	Madonna, Stephen Bray	Madonna, Patrick Leonard, Stephen Bray	4 minutes 21 seconds
6	'True Blue'	Madonna, Stephen Bray	Madonna, Stephen Bray	4 minutes 18 seconds
7	'La Isla Bonita'	Madonna, Patrick Leonard, Bruce Glaitsch	Madonna, Patrick Leonard	4 minutes 2 seconds
8	'Jimmy Jimmy'	Madonna, Stephen Bray	Madonna, Stephen Bray	3 minutes 56 seconds
9	'Love Makes the World Go Round'	Madonna, Patrick Leonard	Madonna, Patrick Leonard	4 minutes 31 seconds

Like a Prayer (1989)

	Title	Writer	Producer	Length
1	'Like a Prayer'	Madonna, Patrick Leonard	Madonna, Patrick Leonard	5 minutes 39 seconds
2	'Express Yourself'	Madonna, Stephen Bray	Madonna, Stephen Bray	4 minutes 39 seconds
3	'Love Song' (featuring Prince)	Madonna, Prince	Madonna, Prince	4 minutes 52 seconds
4	'Till Death Do Us Part'	Madonna, Patrick Leonard	Madonna, Patrick Leonard	5 minutes 16 seconds
5	'Promise to Try'	Madonna, Patrick Leonard	Madonna, Patrick Leonard	3 minutes 36 seconds
6	'Cherish'	Madonna, Patrick Leonard	Madonna, Patrick Leonard	5 minutes 3 seconds
7	'Dear Jessie'	Madonna, Patrick Leonard	Madonna, Patrick Leonard	4 minutes 20 seconds
8	'Oh Father'	Madonna, Patrick Leonard	Madonna, Patrick Leonard	4 minutes 57 seconds
9	'Keep it Together'	Madonna, Stephen Bray	Madonna, Stephen Bray	5 minutes 3 seconds
10	'Spanish Eyes'	Madonna, Patrick Leonard	Madonna, Patrick Leonard	5 minutes 15 seconds
11	'Act of Contrition'	Madonna, Patrick Leonard	Madonna, Patrick Leonard	2 minutes 19 seconds

Erotica (1992)

	Title	Writer	Producer	Length
1	'Erotica'	Madonna, Shep Pettibone, Anthony Shimkin	Madonna, Shep Pettibone	5 minutes 20 seconds
2	'Fever'	Eddie Cooley, John Davenport	Madonna, Shep Pettibone	5 minutes 0 seconds
3	'Bye Bye Baby'	Madonna, Shep Pettibone, Anthony Shimkin	Madonna, Shep Pettibone	3 minutes 56 seconds
4	'Deeper and Deeper'	Madonna, Shep Pettibone, Anthony Shimkin	Madonna, Shep Pettibone	5 minutes 33 seconds
5	'Where Life Begins'	Madonna, André Betts	Madonna, André Betts	5 minutes 57 seconds

6	'Bad Girl'	Madonna, Shep Pettibone, Anthony Shimkin	Madonna, Shep Pettibone	5 minutes 23 seconds
7	'Waiting'	Madonna, André Betts	Madonna, André Betts	5 minutes 46 seconds
8	'Thief of Hearts'	Madonna, Shep Pettibone, Anthony Shimkin	Madonna, Shep Pettibone	4 minutes 51 seconds
9	'Words'	Madonna, Shep Pettibone, Anthony Shimkin	Madonna, Shep Pettibone	5 minutes 55 seconds
10	'Rain'	Madonna, Shep Pettibone	Madonna, Shep Pettibone	5 minutes 25 seconds
11	'Why's It So Hard'	Madonna, Shep Pettibone, Anthony Shimkin	Madonna, Shep Pettibone	5 minutes 23 seconds
12	'In This Life'	Madonna, Shep Pettibone	Madonna, Shep Pettibone	6 minutes 23 seconds
13	'Did You Do It?'	Madonna, Shep Pettibone, André Betts	Madonna, André Betts	4 minutes 54 seconds
14	'Secret Garden'	Madonna, André Betts	Madonna, André Betts	5 minutes 32 seconds

Bedtime Stories (1994)

	Title	Writer	Producer	Length
1	'Survival'	Madonna, Dallas Austin	Nellee Hooper, Madonna	3 minutes 31 seconds
2	'Secret'	Madonna, Dallas Austin	Madonna, Dallas Austin	5 minutes 3 seconds
3	'I'd Rather Be Your Lover'	Madonna, Dave Hall, Isley Brothers, Christopher Jasper	Madonna, Dave Hall	4 minutes 39 seconds
4	'Don't Stop'	Madonna, Dallas Austin, Colin Wolfe	Madonna, Dallas Austin	4 minutes 38 seconds

5	'Inside of Me'	Madonna, Dave Hall, Nellee Hooper	Nellee Hooper, Madonna	4 minutes 11 seconds
6	'Human Nature'	Madonna, Dave Hall, Shawn McKenzie, Kevin McKenzie, Michael Deering	Madonna, Dave Hall	4 minutes 54 seconds
7	'Forbidden Love'	Babyface, Madonna	Nellee Hooper, Madonna	4 minutes 8 seconds
8	'Love Tried to Welcome Me'	Madonna, Dave Hall	Madonna, Dave Hall	5 minutes 21 seconds
9	'Sanctuary'	Madonna, Dallas Austin, Anne Preven, Scott Cutler, Herbie Hancock	Madonna, Dallas Austin	5 minutes 2 seconds
10	'Bedtime Story'	Nellee Hooper, Bjork, Marius DeVries	Nellee Hooper, Madonna	4 minutes 53 seconds
11	'Take a Bow'	Babyface, Madonna	Babyface, Madonna	5 minutes 21 seconds

Ray of Light (1998)

	Title	Writer	Producer	Length
1	'Drowned World'/ 'Substitute for Love'	Madonna, William Orbit, Rod McKuen, Anita Kerr, David Collins	Madonna, William Orbit	5 minutes 9 seconds
2	'Swim'	Madonna, William Orbit	Madonna, William Orbit	5 minutes 0 seconds
3	'Ray of Light'	Madonna, William Orbit, Clive Maldoon, Dave Curtiss, Christine Leach	Madonna, William Orbit	5 minutes 21 seconds

	Title	Writer	Producer	Length
4	'Candy Perfume Girl'	Madonna, William Orbit, Susannah Melvoin	Madonna, William Orbit	4 minutes 34 seconds
5	'Skin'	Madonna, Patrick Leonard	Madonna, William Orbit, Marius DeVries	6 minutes 22 seconds
6	'Nothing Really Matters'	Madonna, Patrick Leonard	Madonna, William Orbit, Marius DeVries	4 minutes 27 seconds
7	'Sky Fits Heaven'	Madonna, Patrick Leonard	Madonna, William Orbit, Patrick Leonard	4 minutes 48 seconds
8	'Shanti/Ashtangi'	Madonna, William Orbit	Madonna, William Orbit	4 minutes 29 seconds
9	'Frozen'	Madonna, Patrick Leonard	Madonna, William Orbit, Patrick Leonard	6 minutes 12 seconds
10	'The Power of Good-Bye'	Madonna, Rick Nowels	Madonna, William Orbit, Patrick Leonard	4 minutes 10 seconds
11	'To Have and Not to Hold'	Madonna, Rick Nowels	Madonna, William Orbit, Patrick Leonard	5 minutes 23 seconds
12	'Little Star'	Madonna, Rick Nowels	Madonna, Marius DeVries	5 minutes 18 seconds
13	'Mer Girl'	Madonna, William Orbit	Madonna, William Orbit	5 minutes 32 seconds

Music (2000)

	Title	Writer	Producer	Length
1	'Music'	Madonna, Mirwais Ahmadzaï	Madonna, Mirwais Ahmadzaï	3 minutes 44 seconds
2	'Impressive Instant'	Madonna, Mirwais Ahmadzaï	Madonna, Mirwais Ahmadzaï	3 minutes 37 seconds
3	'Runaway Lover'	Madonna, William Orbit	Madonna, William Orbit	4 minutes 46 seconds
4	'I Deserve It'	Madonna, Mirwais Ahmadzaï	Madonna, Mirwais Ahmadzaï	4 minutes 23 seconds
5	'Amazing'	Madonna, William Orbit	Madonna, William Orbit	3 minutes 43 seconds

6	'Nobody's Perfect'	Madonna, Mirwais Ahmadzaï	Madonna, Mirwais Ahmadzaï	4 minutes 58 seconds
7	'Don't Tell Me'	Madonna, Mirwais Ahmadzaï, Joe Henry	Madonna, Mirwais Ahmadzaï	4 minutes 58 seconds
8	'What It Feels Like for a Girl'	Madonna, Guy Sigsworth, David Tom	Madonna, Guy Sigsworth, Mark 'Spike' Stent	4 minutes 43 seconds
9	'Paradise (Not for Me)'	Madonna, Mirwais Ahmadzaï	Madonna, Mirwais Ahmadzaï	6 minutes 33 seconds
10	'Gone'	Madonna, Damian Le Gassick, Nik Young	Madonna, William Orbit, Mark 'Spike' Stent	3 minutes 24 seconds

American Life (2003)

	Title	Writer	Producer	Length
1	'American Life'	Madonna, Mirwais Ahmadzaï	Madonna, Mirwais Ahmadzaï	4 minutes 58 seconds
2	'Hollywood'	Madonna, Mirwais Ahmadzaï	Madonna, Mirwais Ahmadzaï	4 minutes 24 seconds
3	'I'm So Stupid'	Madonna, Mirwais Ahmadzaï	Madonna, Mirwais Ahmadzaï, Mark 'Spike' Stent	4 minutes 9 seconds
4	'Love Profusion'	Madonna, Mirwais Ahmadzaï	Madonna, Mirwais Ahmadzaï	3 minutes 38 seconds
5	'Nobody Knows Me'	Madonna, Mirwais Ahmadzaï	Madonna, Mirwais Ahmadzaï	4 minutes 39 seconds
6	'Nothing Fails'	Madonna, Guy Sigsworth, Jem Griffiths	Madonna, Mirwais Ahmadzaï, Mark 'Spike' Stent	4 minutes 49 seconds
7	'Intervention'	Madonna, Mirwais Ahmadzaï	Madonna, Mirwais Ahmadzaï	4 minutes 54 seconds
8	'X-Static Process'	Madonna, Stuart Price	Madonna, Mirwais Ahmadzaï	3 minutes 50 seconds

9	'Mother and Father'	Madonna, Mirwais Ahmadzaï	Madonna, Mirwais Ahmadzaï	4 minutes 33 seconds
10	'Die Another Day'	Madonna, Mirwais Ahmadzaï	Madonna, Mirwais Ahmadzaï	4 minutes 38 seconds
11	'Easy Ride'	Madonna, Monte Pittman	Madonna, Mirwais Ahmadzaï	5 minutes 5 seconds

Confessions on a Dance Floor (2005)

	Title	Writer	Producer	Length
1	'Hung Up'	Madonna, Stuart Price, Benny Andersson, Bjorn Ulvaeus	Madonna, Stuart Price	5 minutes 36 seconds
2	'Get Together'	Madonna, Anders Bagge, Peer Astrom, Stuart Price	Madonna, Stuart Price	5 minutes 30 seconds
3	'Sorry'	Madonna, Stuart Price	Madonna, Stuart Price	4 minutes 43 seconds
4	'Future Lovers'	Madonna, Mirwais Ahmadzaï	Madonna, Mirwais Ahmadzaï	4 minutes 51 seconds
5	'I Love New York'	Madonna, Stuart Price	Madonna, Stuart Price	4 minutes 11 seconds
6	'Let It Will Be'	Madonna, Mirwais Ahmadzaï, Stuart Price	Madonna, Stuart Price	4 minutes 18 seconds
7	'Forbidden Love'	Madonna, Stuart Price	Madonna, Stuart Price	4 minutes 22 seconds
8	'Jump'	Madonna, Joe Henry, Stuart Price	Madonna, Stuart Price	3 minutes 46 seconds
9	'How High'	Madonna, Christian Karlsson, Pontus Winnberg, Henrik Jonback	Madonna, Christian Karlsson, Pontus Winnberg, Stuart Price	4 minutes 40 seconds

10	'Isaac'	Madonna, Stuart Price	Madonna, Stuart Price	6 minutes 3 seconds
11	'Push'	Madonna, Stuart Price	Madonna, Stuart Price	3 minutes 57 seconds
12	'Like It or Not'	Madonna, Christian Karlsson, Pontus Winnberg, Henrik Jonback	Madonna, Christian Karlsson, Pontus Winnberg	4 minutes 31 seconds

Hard Candy (2008)

	Title	Writer	Producer	Length
1	'Candy Shop'	Pharrell Williams, Madonna	The Neptunes (i.e. Pharrell Williams and Chad Hugo), Madonna	4 minutes 16 seconds
2	'4 Minutes' (featuring Justin Timberlake and Timbaland)	Madonna, Tim Mosley, Justin Timberlake, Nate Hills	Timbaland, Justin Timberlake, Danja	4 minutes 4 seconds
3	'Give It 2 Me'	Pharrell Williams, Madonna	The Neptunes, Madonna	4 minutes 48 seconds
4	'Heartbeat'	Pharrell Williams, Madonna	The Neptunes, Madonna	4 minutes 4 seconds
5	'Miles Away'	Madonna, Tim Mosley, Justin Timberlake, Nate Hills	Timbaland, Justin Timberlake, Danja	4 minutes 49 seconds
6	'She's Not Me'	Pharrell Williams, Madonna	The Neptunes, Madonna	6 minutes 5 seconds
7	'Incredible'	Pharrell Williams, Madonna	The Neptunes, Madonna	6 minutes 20 seconds
8	'Beat Goes On' (featuring Kanye West)	Pharrell Williams, Madonna, Kanye West	The Neptunes, Madonna	4 minutes 27 seconds

9	'Dance 2night' (featuring Justin Timberlake)	Madonna, Tim Mosley, Justin Timberlake, Hannon Lane	Timbaland, Justin Timberlake, Hannon Lane, Demo Castellon	5 minutes 3 seconds
10	'Spanish Lesson'	Pharrell Williams, Madonna	The Neptunes, Madonna	3 minutes 38 seconds
11	'Devil Wouldn't Recognize You'	Madonna, Tim Mosley, Timberlake, Nate Hills, Joe Henry	Timbaland, Justin Timberlake, Dania	5 minutes 9 seconds
12	'Voices'	Madonna, Tim Mosley, Justin Timberlake, Nate Hills, Hannon Lane	Timbaland, Justin Timberlake, Dania, Hannon Lane	3 minutes 29 seconds

MDNA (2012)

	Title	Writer	Producer	Length
1	'Girl Gone Wild'	Madonna, Jenson Vaughan, Alle Benassi, Benny Benassi	Madonna, Alle Benassi, Benny Benassi	3 minutes 44 seconds
2	'Gang Bang'	Madonna, William Orbit, Priscilla Hamilton, Keith Harris, Jean Baptiste, Mika, Don Juan Demo Casanova, Stephen Kozmeniuk	Madonna, William Orbit, Demolition Crew	5 minutes 28 seconds
3	'I'm Addicted'	Madonna, Alle Benassi, Benny Benassi	Madonna, Alle Benassi, Benny Benassi	4 minutes 34 seconds
4	'Turn Up the Radio'	Madonna, Martin Solveig, Michael Tordjman, Jade Williams	Madonna, Martin Solveig	3 minutes 48 seconds

5	'Give Me All Your Luvin' (featuring Nicki Minaj and M.I.A.)	Madonna, Martin Solveig, Nicki Minaj, Maya Arulpragasam, Michael Tordjman	Madonna, Martin Solveig	3 minutes 22 seconds
6	'Some Girls'	Madonna, William Orbit, Klas Ahlund	Madonna, William Orbit, Klas Ahlund	4 minutes 55 seconds
7	'Superstar'	Madonna, Indiigo	Madonna, Indiigo, Michael Malih	3 minutes 53 seconds
8	'I Don't Give A' (featuring Nicki Minaj)	Madonna, Martin Solveig, Nicki Minaj, Julien Jabre	Madonna, Martin Solveig	4 minutes 21 seconds
9	'I'm a Sinner'	Madonna, William Orbit, Jean Baptiste	Madonna, William Orbit	4 minutes 52 seconds
10	'Love Spent'	Madonna, William Orbit, Jean Baptiste, Priscilla Hamilton, Alain Whyte, Ryan Buendia, Michael McHenry	Madonna, William Orbit	3 minutes 45 seconds
11	'Masterpiece'	Madonna, Julie Frost, Jimmy Harry	Madonna, William Orbit	4 minutes 0 seconds
12	'Falling Free'	Madonna, Laurie Mayaer, William Orbit, Joe Henry	Madonna, William Orbit	5 minutes 12 seconds

A BRIEF ETYMOLOGICAL INTERLUDE

Engagement

From 'engage' + 'ment'. 'Engage' is from the Old French *en* (make) and *gage* (pledge), which taken together came to mean 'to pledge' from the early fifteenth century onwards; '-ment' is from a Latin suffix, *-mentum*, which was added to the stems of verbs to represent the product or result of an action.

Fiancé

From the French *fiancé*, which is the past participle of *fiancer* (to betroth), from the noun *fiancé* (a promise or a trust), which itself is a derivation of *fier* (to trust) from the Latin verb *fidare*. Noble though its origins are, however, more elegant terms for this particular relationship include 'my intended' or 'my betrothed'.

Heart

From the Old English word *heorte*, which comes from *herta* in Old Saxon, *herte* in Old Frisian, *hjarta* in Old Norse and *khertan* in Proto-Germanic.

Banns

From the Old English word *bannan* (to proclaim, command or summon).

Bride

From the Old English term *bryd* (bride, newly married woman), which comes from words like *bruthiz* in Proto-Germanic, *breid* in Old Frisian, *bruid* in Dutch and *brut* in Old High German. However, the similar term *bruþs* in Gothic, and later *bruta* in medieval Latin and *bruy* in Old French, specifically referred to a daughter-in-law, since custom in most ancient cultures decreed that a married woman lived with her husband's family.

Groom

From the Old English *brydguma* (suitor), an amalgamation of *bryd* (bride) and *guma* (man). Most languages of similar Germanic origin also utilize this compound — *bryd* in Old Saxon, *bruðgumi* in Old Norse, *brutigomo* in Old High German — except for Gothic, which used *bruþsfaþs* (bride's lord).

Wedding

The original term for this was *bridelope* (bridal run), which referred to a bride being escorted from her old home, where she used to live with her parents, to her new home, where she was to live with her husband. *Bridelope!* So brilliant. From about 1300 onwards the Old English *weddung* (state of being wed) was more commonly used, boringly. This word goes way back: *weddian* (to pledge) in Old English, *wadjojanan* (to pledge) in Proto-Germanic, *veðja* (to bet) in Old Norse, *weddia* (to promise) in Old Frisian, which in turn all come from the Latin *vadis* (bail, security).

Kiss

From the Old English *cyssan* (to kiss), which derives from *kussijanan* in Proto-Germanic, *kyssa* in Old Norse, *kessa* in Old Frisian, *kussian* in Old Saxon and so on. Probably all come from imitating the sound of the action in question.

Husband

Early on, the Old English term was *wer* (married man), but from the late thirteenth century onwards this was gradually replaced by *husbonda* (male head of the household), the derivation of which is evident in the Old Norse terms *hus* (house) and *bondi* (dweller, peasant). Interestingly, the slang term *hubby* can be found as far back as the 1680s.

Wife

From the Old English word *wif* (woman), which has a relatively straightforward derivation from *wif* in Old Saxon and Old Frisian, *wiban* in Proto-Germanic and so on. Thus being a wife and being a woman were inextricably intertwined in that period.

Honeymoon

The term *honymoone* dates back to the mid-sixteenth century, referring to the period immediately after a couple have got married. One can only speculate as to why: perhaps because it is a period as sweet as honey which lasts only as long as a month's lunar cycle? In French it is *lune de miel*, in German *Flitterwochen*, which literally translates as 'tinsel week', rather wonderfully. It was only in the early nineteenth century that the word came to refer specifically to a holiday that followed the wedding festivities.

Bed

From the Old English word *bedd*, which comes from *badjam* (a place to sleep dug in the ground) in Proto-Germanic. The root is the Proto-Indo-European term *bhedh* (to dig or pierce).

Marriage

Little of interest to report here, unfortunately — linguistically at least. This Middle English word first appears in around 1300 and came from *marier* (to marry) in Old French and before that from *maritare* (to get married) in Latin.

Happy

In almost all European languages, the word for 'happy' originally meant 'lucky' — except in Welsh, where it meant 'wise'. 'Happy' comes from *hap* (chance, fortune, fate), from *happ* in Old Norse and *khapan* in Proto-Germanic. Its current sense is first recorded in the late fourteenth century.

Argue

Its current meaning originates in the late fourteenth century and comes from the Old French *arguer* (to maintain an opinion or view), which in turn comes from the Latin *arguere* (to prove, declare, demonstrate, make clear), from the Proto-Indo-European root *arg-* (to be clear/bright/white or to shine).

Compromise

From the thirteenth-century Middle French word *compromis*, which derives from the Latin *compromissus*, which is the past participle of *compromittere* (*com* and *promittere*, 'together' and 'to promise').

WHOM NOT TO MARRY

IN 1560, the Church of England compiled a list of marriages that were forbidden, according to either the Bible or to the English law, or to both, which remained unchanged until well into the twentieth century.[1] Study it carefully. You do not want any nasty surprises, after all, just in case you are indeed in a hazy love match with your sister's daughter's husband or the like. Best to be sure.

A man may not marry his . . .	A woman may not marry her . . .
Grandmother	Grandfather
Grandfather's wife (i.e. stepgrandmother)	Grandmother's husband (i.e. stepgrandfather)
Wife's grandmother (i.e. grandmother-in-law)	Husband's grandfather (i.e. grandfather-in-law)
Father's sister (i.e. aunt)	Father's brother (i.e. uncle)
Mother's sister (i.e. aunt)	Mother's brother (i.e. uncle)

A man may not marry his . . .	*A woman may not marry her . . .*
Father's brother's wife (i.e. aunt-in-law)	Father's sister's husband (i.e. uncle-in-law)
Mother's brother's wife (i.e. aunt-in-law)	Mother's sister's husband (i.e. uncle-in-law)
Wife's father's sister (i.e. aunt-in-law)	Husband's father's brother (i.e. uncle-in-law)
Wife's mother's sister (i.e. aunt-in-law)	Husband's mother's brother (i.e. uncle-in-law)
Mother	Father
Stepmother	Stepfather
Wife's mother (i.e. mother-in-law)	Husband's father ((i.e. father-in-law)
Daughter	Son
Wife's daughter (i.e. stepdaughter)	Husband's son (i.e. stepson)
Son's wife (i.e. daughter-in-law)	Daughter's husband (i.e. son-in-law)
Sister	Brother
Wife's sister (i.e. sister-in-law)	Husband's brother (i.e. brother-in-law)
Brother's wife (i.e. sister-in-law)	Sister's husband (i.e. brother-in-law)
Son's daughter (i.e. granddaughter)	Son's son (i.e. grandson)
Daughter's daughter (i.e. granddaughter)	Daughter's son (i.e. grandson)
Son's son's wife (i.e. granddaughter-in-law)	Son's daughter's husband (i.e. grandson-in-law)
Daughter's son's wife (i.e. granddaughter-in-law)	Daughter's daughter's husband (i.e. grandson-in-law)
Wife's son's daughter (i.e. stepgranddaughter)	Husband's son's son (i.e. stepgrandson)
Wife's daughter's daughter (i.e. stepgranddaughter)	Husband's daughter's son (i.e. stepgrandson)
Brother's daughter (i.e. niece)	Brother's son (i.e. nephew)
Sister's daughter (i.e. niece)	Sister's son (i.e. nephew)
Brother's son's wife (i.e. niece-in-law)	Brother's daughter's husband (i.e. nephew-in-law)
Sister's son's wife (i.e. niece-in-law)	Sister's daughter's husband (i.e. nephew-in-law)
Wife's brother's daughter (i.e. niece-in-law)	Husband's brother's son (i.e. nephew-in-law)
Wife's sister's daughter (i.e. niece-in-law)	Husband's sister's son (i.e. nephew-in-law)

1   Over the course of the twentieth century, various restrictions were added and removed:

- · The 1907 Marriage Act allowed one to marry one's wife's sister or husband's
  brother, as long as the first spouse in each case was already dead.
- · The 1921 Marriage Act allowed one to marry one's brother's wife or sister's husband,
  as long as the sibling in each case was already dead.
- · The 1931 Marriage Act allowed one to marry one's aunt-in-law, uncle-in-law,
  niece-in-law or nephew-in-law, as long as the relevant uncle, aunt, niece or nephew
  was already dead. This last restriction was removed, however, by the 1960 Marriage
  Act, so that divorcees in this category were able to remarry.

Finally, recently introduced rules prevent a man from marrying his adoptive mother or
adopted daughter and a woman from marrying her adoptive father or adopted son.

DARWIN ON MARRIAGE

HAVING last-minute doubts? Is your betrothed having last-minute doubts? Here is one man's thoughts on the subject: Charles Darwin's, to be precise, in a note he scribbled to himself in July 1838.

This is the Question

Marry

Children—(if it Please God)—Constant companion, (& friend in old age) who will feel interested in one,—object to be beloved & played with.— —better than a dog anyhow.[2]— Home, & someone to take care of house—Charms of music & female chit-chat.—These things good for one's health.— *but terrible loss of time.—*

---

2   Thanks, Charles. How charming.

My God, it is intolerable to think of spending ones whole life, like a neuter bee, working, working, & nothing after all.—No, no won't do.—Imagine living all one's day solitarily in smoky dirty London House.—Only picture to yourself a nice soft wife on a sofa with good fire, & books & music perhaps— Compare this vision with the dingy reality of Grt. Marlbro' St.

Marry—Marry—Marry Q.E.D.

Not Marry

Freedom to go where one liked—choice of Society & *little of it.*— Conversation of clever men at clubs—Not forced to visit relatives, & to bend in every trifle.—to have the expense & anxiety of children— perhaps quarelling—Loss of time.—cannot read in the Evenings—fatness & idleness—Anxiety & responsibility—less money for books &c—if many children forced to gain one's bread.—(But then it is very bad for ones health to work too much)

Perhaps my wife wont like London; then the sentence is banishment & degradation into indolent, idle fool—

It being proved necessary to Marry

When? Soon or Late

The Governor says soon for otherwise bad if one has children— one's character is more flexible—one's feelings more lively & if one does not marry soon, one misses so much good pure happiness.—

But then if I married tomorrow: there would be an infinity of trouble & expense in getting & furnishing a house,—fighting about no Society—morning calls—awkwardness—loss of time every day. (without one's wife was an angel, & made one keep industrious). Then how should I manage all my business if I were obliged to go every day walking with my wife.—Eheu!! I never should know French,—or see the Continent—or go to America, or go up in a Balloon, or take solitary trip in Wales— poor slave.—you will be worse than a negro— And then horrid poverty, (without one's wife was better than an angel & had money)—Never mind my boy—Cheer up—One cannot live this solitary life, with groggy old age, friendless & cold, & childless staring one in ones face, already beginning to wrinkle.—Never mind, trust to chance—keep a sharp look out—There is many a happy slave—

Darwin did indeed propose to his cousin Emma in November 1838; they were married the following January, and went on to live happily ever after.

MARRIAGE CEREMONIES IN ENGLAND AND WALE

Selected years[1]	Total number of marriages	With civil ceremonies	With religious ceremonies
			All
2010	243,808	165,680	78,128
2009	232,443	155,950	76,493
2008	235,794	157,296	78,498
2007	235,367	156,198	79,169
2006	239,454	158,350	81,104
2005	247,805	162,169	85,636
2004	273,069	184,913	88,156
2003	270,109	183,124	86,985
2002	255,596	169,210	86,386
2001	249,227	160,238	88,989
2000	267,961	170,800	97,161
1999	263,515	162,679	100,836
1998	267,303	163,072	104,231
1997	272,536	165,516	107,020
1996	278,975	164,158	114,817
1995	283,012	155,490	127,522
1994	291,069	152,113	138,956
1993	299,197	152,930	146,267
1992	311,564	156,967	154,597
1991	306,756	151,333	155,423
1990	331,150	156,875	174,275
1989	346,697	166,651	180,046
1988	348,492	168,897	179,595
1987	351,761	168,190	183,571
1986	347,924	168,255	179,669
1985	346,389	169,025	177,364
1984	349,186	170,506	178,680
1983	344,334	167,327	177,007
1982	342,166	165,089	177,077
1981	351,973	172,514	179,459
1980	370,022	183,395	186,627
1979	368,853	187,381	181,472
1978	368,258	186,239	182,019
1977	356,954	180,446	176,508
1976	358,567	179,330	179,237
1975	380,620	181,824	198,796
1974	384,389	178,710	205,679
1973	400,435	184,724	215,711

BY TYPE AND DENOMINATION (1837–2010)

Church of England and Church in Wales	Roman Catholic	Other Christian denominations[2]	Other[3]
57,607	8,622	9,032	2,867
56,236	8,426	8,973	2,858
57,057	8,909	9,745	2,787
57,101	8,904	10,351	2,813
57,963	9,263	11,249	2,629
61,155	9,599	12,315	2,567
62,006	9,850	13,578	2,722
60,385	9,858	14,188	2,554
58,980	10,044	14,844	2,518
60,878	10,518	15,210	2,383
65,536	11,312	17,751	2,562
67,219	12,399	18,690	2,528
69,494	12,615	19,746	2,376
70,310	13,125	21,211	2,374
75,147	13,989	23,605	2,076
83,685	15,181	26,622	2,034
90,703	16,429	29,807	2,017
96,060	17,465	30,804	1,938
101,883	18,795	32,006	1,913
102,840	19,551	31,069	1,963
11̶5̶,̶?̶?̶8̶	?̶?̶,̶?̶6̶6̶	?̶4̶,̶6̶?̶?̶	1̶,̶8̶?̶?̶
118,956	23,737	35,551	1,802
118,423	24,372	34,975	1,825
121,293	25,020	35,589	1,669
117,804	24,578	35,507	1,780
116,378	25,207	33,938	1,841
117,506	25,609	33,866	1,699
116,854	25,211	33,252	1,690
116,978	24,834	33,835	1,430
?̶?̶0̶,̶?̶?̶?̶	?̶?̶,̶?̶?̶?̶	?̶?̶,̶?̶?̶?̶	1̶,̶?̶?̶?̶
123,400	28,553	33,164	1,510
119,420	28,477	32,007	1,568
119,970	28,654	31,882	1,513
116,749	28,204	30,008	1,547
119,569	28,714	29,462	1,492
133,074	32,307	31,845	1,570
137,767	33,702	34,210[4]	
143,853	36,267	35,591	

Selected years[1]	Total number of marriages	With civil ceremonies	With religious ceremonies
			All
1972	426,241	194,134	232,107
1971	404,737	167,101	237,636
1970	415,487	164,119	251,368
1969	396,746	143,115	253,631
1968	407,822	144,572	263,250
1967	386,052	131,576	254,476
1966	384,497	127,502	256,995
1965	371,127	118,034	253,093
1964	359,307	111,053	248,254
1963	351,329	107,384	243,945
1962	347,732	103,102	244,630
1957	346,903	97,084	249,819
1952	349,308	106,777	242,531
1934	342,307	97,120	245,187
1929	313,316	80,475	232,841
1924	296,416	70,604	225,812
1919	369,411	85,330	284,081
1914	294,401	70,880	223,521
1913	286,583	62,328	224,255
1912	283,834	58,367	225,467
1911	274,943	57,435	217,508
1910	267,721	54,678	213,043
1909	260,544	53,505	207,039
1908	264,940	54,048	210,892
1907	276,421	54,026	222,395
1906	270,038	50,682	219,356
1905	260,742	47,768	212,974
1904	257,856	46,247	211,609
1903	261,103	44,520	216,583
1902	261,750	42,761	218,989
1901	259,400	41,067	218,333
1900	257,480	39,471	218,009
1899	262,334	39,403	222,931
1898	255,379	37,938	217,441
1897	249,145	36,626	212,519
1896	242,764	35,439	207,325
1895	228,204	33,749	194,455
1894	226,449	33,550	192,899
1893	218,689	31,379	187,310
1892	227,135	31,416	195,719
1891	226,526	30,809	195,717

Church of England and Church in Wales	Roman Catholic	Other Christian denominations[2] Other[3]
155,538	39,694	36,875
160,165	41,399	36,072
170,146	43,658	37,564
172,067	43,441	38,123
178,700	44,931	39,619
173,278	43,305	37,893
175,254	43,814	37,927
171,848	43,192	38,053
167,742	42,525	37,987
163,837	42,272	37,836
164,707	42,788	37,135
172,010	39,960	37,849
173,282	33,050	26,199
183,123	22,323	39,741
176,113	18,711	38,017
171,480	16,286	38,046
220,557	19,078	44,446
171,700	13,729	38,092
172,640	13,349	38,266
174,357	12,715	38,395
167,925	12,002	37,581
164,945	11,312	36,786
159,991	10,962	36,086
163,086	10,910	36,066
172,497	11,700	38,198
170,579	11,455	37,322
165,747	10,812	36,415
165,519	10,450	35,640
170,044	10,621	35,918
173,011	10,606	35,372
172,679	10,624	35,030
173,060	10,267	34,682
177,896	10,686	34,349
174,826	10,164	32,451
170,806	10,095	31,618
166,871	10,042	30,412
156,469	9,405	28,581
155,352	9,453	28,094
151,309	9,019	26,982
158,632	9,133	27,954
158,439	9,517	27,761

Selected years[1]	Total number of marriages	With civil ceremonies	With religious ceremonies
			All
1890	223,028	30,376	192,652
1889	213,865	29,779	184,086
1888	203,821	27,809	176,012
1887	200,518	27,335	173,183
1886	196,071	25,590	170,481
1885	197,745	25,851	171,894
1884	204,301	26,786	177,515
1883	206,384	26,547	179,837
1882	204,405	25,717	178,688
1881	197,290	25,055	172,235
1880	191,965	24,180	167,785
1879	182,082	21,769	160,313
1878	190,054	22,056	167,998
1877	194,352	21,269	173,083
1876	201,874	21,709	180,165
1875	201,212	21,002	180,210
1874	202,010	21,256	180,754
1873	205,615	21,178	184,437
1872	201,267	19,995	181,272
1871	190,112	18,378	171,734
1870	181,655	17,848	163,807
1869	176,970	16,745	160,225
1868	176,962	15,878	161,084
1867	179,154	15,058	164,096
1866	187,776	15,246	172,530
1865	185,474	14,792	170,682
1864	180,387	14,611	165,776
1863	173,510	13,589	159,921
1862	164,030	12,723	151,307
1861	163,706	11,725	151,981
1860	170,156	11,257	158,899
1859	167,723	10,844	156,879
1858	156,070	9,952	146,118
1857	159,097	9,642	149,455
1856	159,337	8,097	151,240
1855	152,113	7,441	144,672
1854	159,727	7,593	152,134
1853	164,520	7,598	156,922
1852	158,782	7,100	151,682
1851	154,206	6,813	147,393
1850	152,744	6,207	146,537

Church of England and Church in Wales	Roman Catholic	Other Christian denominations[2] Other[3]
156,371	9,596	26,685
149,356	8,988	25,742
142,863	8,632	24,517
140,607	8,611	23,965
138,571	8,220	23,690
139,913	8,162	23,819
144,344	8,783	24,388
147,000	8,980	23,857
146,102	9,235	23,351
140,995	8,784	22,456
137,661	8,210	21,914
131,689	7,437	21,187
137,969	7,980	22,049
142,396	8,277	22,410
148,910	8,577	22,678
149,685	8,411	22,114
150,819	8,179	21,756
154,581	8,222	21,634
152,364	8,427	20,481
144,663	7,647	19,424
137,986	7,391	18,430
135,082	7,231	17,912
136,038	7,517	17,529
148,000	7,918	17,248
146,040	8,911	17,579
145,104	8,742	16,836
141,083	8,659	16,034
136,743	8,095	15,083
129,733	7,345	14,229
130,697	7,782	13,502
137,370	7,800	13,729
136,210	7,756	12,913
128,082	6,643	11,393
131,031	7,360	11,064
133,619	7,527	10,094
127,751	7,344	9,577
134,109	7,813	10,212
138,042	8,375	10,505
133,882	7,479	10,321
130,958	6,570	9,865
130,959	5,623	9,955

Selected years[1]	Total number of marriages	With civil ceremonies	With religious ceremonies
			All
1849	141,883	5,558	136,325
1848	138,230	4,790	133,440
1847	135,845	4,258	131,587
1846	145,664	4,167	141,497
1845	143,743	3,977	139,766
1844	132,249	3,446	128,803
1843	123,818	2,817	121,001
1842	118,825	2,357	116,468
1841	122,496	2,064	120,323
1841 – year ending 30 June	122,482	2,036	120,446
1840 – year ending 30 June	124,329	1,938	122,391
1839 – year ending 30 June	121,083	1,564	119,519
1838 – year ending 30 June	111,481	1,093	110,388
1837 – 1 July–31 December	58,479	431	58,048

---

1 Data are not available for years not shown.

2 'Other Christian denominations' include Methodist, Calvinistic Methodist, United Reform Church, Congregationalist, Baptist, Presbyterian, Society of Friends (Quakers), Salvation Army, Brethren, Mormon, Unitarian and Jehovah's Witnesses.

3 'Other' include Jews, Muslims and Sikhs.

4 Prior to 1975 further information on denominations was not published.

Church of England and *Church in Wales*	*Roman Catholic*	*Other Christian denominations*[2]	*Other*[3]
123,182	4,199	8,944	
121,469	3,658	8,313	
120,876	2,961	7,750	
130,509	3,027	7,961	
129,515	2,816	7,435	
120,009	2,280	6,514	
113,637	7,213	151	
110,047	6,258	163	
114,371	5,948	113	
114,448	5,882	116	
117,018	5,221	152	
114,632	4,727	160	
107,201	3,052	135	
56,832	1,142	74	

Source: Office for National Statistics

SPOTS, AND HOW TO ATTACK THEM

WHAT the . . . ? How the . . . ? Oh, so mean! Given the established correlation between spots and stress (since stress is known to bring about hormonal fluctuations), it stands to reason that an event like a wedding frequently results in the appearance of at least one of these unsightly blighters, despite the fact that in all likelihood one has not graced your face for over ten years.

Certain 'professionals' condone a bit of a squeeze, if your new friend has matured enough to boast an obvious white head. Before attempting the task, ensure your hands are scrupulously clean, and for heaven's sake, cloak your fingers in tissue, in order to avoid nail damage. Stop squeezing before any blood pops out, as often this results in a flow that feels unstaunchable – particularly if you are rushing around and blood pressure is elevated. Apply a tincture of diluted tea tree oil or an antiseptic cream atop the resultant crater to minimize the risk of infection.

If you are – oh, horror of horrors! – confronted with a spot the evening before the Big Day, get going with some salicylic acid on the end of a cotton bud. This ingredient is present in differing strengths in many over-the-counter zit busters. After cleansing the target area, dab on a bit of toner suffused with alcohol (which will dry up the spot more quickly). Stun him with a bit of hot water, then apply a cotton bud laced with your salicylic acid-containing product of choice until liberally covered. This will no doubt sting, and you should not keep the acid applied for too long; but with luck, by morning a significant reduction in the beaconish quality of the evil appendage will be noticeable. Applying a little tooth-paste to the spot upon waking is another suggested method of attack.

To reduce the odds of the occurrence of such a calamity, in the fortnight leading up to the Big Day drink gallons of water, chomp away on pounds of fruit, and avoid facials which, though seeming luxurious, often involve cleansers and chemicals at which your skin may baulk (unless you are in the habit of having them on a weekly basis). A facial can cause you to look rather blotchy, quite apart from suffering the spotty breakouts it might engender. Steer equally clear of peels or scrubs. Even if they technically leave your complexion blooming at the lower dermal layers, on top you could easily resemble a burns victim. Which is presumably not part of the plan?

QUEEN VICTORIA'S WEDDING DAY: THE ACCOUNT OF ONE OF QUEEN VICTORIA'S BRIDESMAIDS, LADY WILHELMINA STANHOPE, LATER THE DUCHESS OF CLEVELAND

The day proved very rainy early in the morning, but it cleared up at about eleven, and the sun shone out brightly upon the bride as she passed through the rooms with her procession on her way to the chapel.

The procession was thus formed:

THE QUEEN

Left	*Right*
Lady Adelaide Paget	Lady Caroline Lennox
Lady Sarah Villiers	Lady Elizabeth Howard
Lady Fanny Cowper	Lady Ida Hay
Lady Elizabeth West	Lady Wilhelmina Stanhope
Lady Mary Grimston	Lady Jane Bouverie
Lady Mary Howard	Lady Eleanor Paget

I arrived about eleven with my *pendant*, Elizabeth West. Our orders were to go and lock ourselves up in the Queen's dressing-room till she arrived; and accordingly Lord Erroll, whom we found at the foot of the staircase, gave us in charge to a Mr. Dobel, who, to our horror, marshalled us through the state rooms, filled with people waiting to see the procession — some, as I am told, having been sitting there since half-past eight!

The dressing-room, where the twelve young ladies in tulle and white roses were immured for one hour and a half, fortunately commanded a view of the park, and we spent our time in watching the lines of Foot Guards forming under our windows, the evolutions of the Blues, who looked a good deal rusted by the rain, the people in the park, etc.

At about half-past twelve the Queen arrived, looking as white as a sheet, but not apparently nervous. She was dressed in white satin and Honiton lace, with the collars of her orders, which are very splendid, round her neck, and on her head a very high wreath of orange flowers, a very few diamonds studded into her hair behind, in which was fastened her veil, also, I believe, of Honiton lace, and very handsome.

Her train was of white satin, trimmed with orange flowers, but rather too short for the number of young ladies who carried it. We were all huddled together, and scrambled rather than walked along, kicking each other's heels and treading on each other's gowns.

The Queen was perfectly composed and quiet, but unusually pale. She walked very slowly, giving ample time for all the spectators to gratify their curiosity, and certainly she was never before more earnestly scrutinized.

I thought she trembled a little as she entered the chapel, where Prince Albert, the Queen Dowager, and all the royal family were waiting for her. She took her place on the left side of the altar, and knelt down in prayer for a few minutes, and Prince Albert followed her example. He wore a field-marshal's uniform, and two large white satin rosettes on his shoulders, with the Garter, etc. Perhaps he appeared awkward from embarrassment, but he was certainly a good deal perplexed and agitated in delivering his responses.

Her Majesty was quite calm and composed. When Prince Albert was asked whether he would take this woman for his wife, she turned full round and looked into his face as he replied '*I will*.'

Her own responses were given in the same clear, musical tone of voice with which she read her speeches in the House of Lords, and in much the same manner.

The Duke of Sussex was greatly affected, and Lord Fitzwilliam was heard to sob responsively from the gallery, but no one else seemed in the least disturbed. The Duke of Sussex has a story that no one cried but one of the singing boys; however, I can vouch for *his* tears. The Queen's two tears, mentioned in the *Morning Post*, I did not see.

The old Duke of Cambridge was decidedly gay, making very audible remarks from time to time. The Queen Dowager looked quite the beau-ideal of a Queen Dowager — grave, dignified, and very becomingly dressed in purple velvet and ermine, and a purple velvet *coiffure* with a magnificent diamond branch.

After it was over we all filed out of the chapel in the same order, the Duke of Cambridge very gallantly handing the princesses down the steps with many audible civilities. The Queen gave her hand to her husband, who led her back through the rooms (where her reception was enthusiastic) to the throne room, where the royal family, the Coburgs, etc., signed their names in the registry book.

The Queen then presented each of her bridesmaids with a brooch, an eagle (Prince Albert's crest) of turquoise and pearls. After this she took her departure down the back stairs, at the foot of which I consigned the train to Prince Albert's care, who seemed a little nervous about getting into the carriage with a lady with a tail six yards long and voluminous in proportion!

WE ARE GATHERED HERE TODAY . . .

THE wedding ceremony itself can be an intensely strange, surreal experience for the bride and groom. You have seen it happen so many times on screen that you almost feel as though you are in a film yourself — not least because it is one of the very few occasions in life when you are expected to appear all serious and proper, looking your intended right in the eye, without pulling a silly face for even a second in the hope of dispelling the tension. Offered here, however, is a solution: anagrams of the opening phrase of most wedding ceremonies, 'We are gathered here today', that will bring out childish giggles in the best of us and banish any nerves once and for all. Be warned, though: you will never attend a wedding ceremony again without having to stop yourself from laughing at the mental image of 'a greathearted weedy hero' . . .

A greathearted weedy hero
A headgear retorted hey we
A hardhearted eye grew toe
Awarded heat here tee orgy
A tetrahedra hedgerow eye
A hardhearted ewe grey toe
A headgear retorted eh yew
Awarded earth here
A hardhearted ewe goer yet
A headgear deer they wrote
Greathearted ahoy weeder
Awarded are hetero get hey
A hardhearted wee ego tyre
Aerated dowager here they

A headgear wed tree theory
Awarded tea here thee orgy
A hardhearted wee ogre yet
Adage earth wed ere her toy
A headgear reword thee yet
A hardhearted wee goer yet
Awarded earth here ego yet
A headgear rowed there yet
A hardhearted ewe ogre yet
Tetrahedra yeah gored ewe
A headgear owed thee terry
Awarded tea regret hoe hey
A headgear wed eh retro yet
Awarded tea three ogre hey
A greathearted eyed whore

There is also an excellent parlour game to be had in trying to construct a scene from a novel that incorporates one of these phrases. For example:

A headgear retorted, 'Eh! Yew!'
   'Why is that abandoned motorbike helmet talking to that tree?' I wondered suspiciously as I made my way through the forest.

Or:

First, I was awarded tea. 'Here thee orgy!' read a sign on the wall.
   'Oh, so this is where I have the sex party once I've finished this cuppa,' I thought to myself.

Ridiculous as can be, but guaranteed to ease the tension in the moments before you take the final plunge into wedlock.

THE WEDDING MARCH VS 'HERE COMES THE BRIDE'

AN assessment of the two most famous wedding marches in European music – Mendelssohn's Wedding March and Wagner's Bridal Chorus, more commonly known as 'Here Comes the Bride' – takes one into the surprising realms of cultural politics in 1840s Saxony and the history of German anti-Semitism in the nineteenth century. Read on . . .

Both pieces of music were composed in the two largest German cities during the 1840s. Felix Mendelssohn–Bartholdy (1809–47) was at the height of his fame and fairly near the end of his short life when he wrote the incidental music for an 1843 Potsdam production of Shakespeare's *A Midsummer Night's Dream*, in the German version by Schlegel. Mendelssohn came from a famous Jewish family (his grandfather was the philosopher Moses Mendelssohn) but had been baptized as a Lutheran Christian. Shakespeare was probably of particular interest to Mendelssohn given his close links with Britain: he travelled there ten times, and was a favourite composer of Queen Victoria and Prince Albert. His oratorio *Elijah* was premiered in Birmingham, just a short distance from Shakespeare's birthplace and his Forest of Arden.

Mendelssohn wrote the music for *A Midsummer Night's Dream* in Leipzig, where he was the Kapellmeister (main conductor and director of music) of the famous Gewandhaus Orchestra. The Wedding March accompanies the wedding of the four lovers, and was designed by Mendelssohn to come between Shakespeare's Acts 4 and 5. The music was presumably inspired partly by Theseus's speech at the end of Act 4:

Fair lovers, you are fortunately met;
Of this discourse we will hear more anon.
Egeus, I will overbear your will;
For in the temple, by and by, with us,
These couples shall be eternally knit.
And, for the morning now is something worn,
Our purpos'd hunting shall be set aside.
Away, with us, to Athens: three and three, we'll hold a feast in
   great solemnity.

Meanwhile, Richard Wagner (1813–83) held a more junior conducting position at the court opera in Dresden. Wagner's talent and career developed much more slowly than Mendelssohn's, and Wagner was always envious and resentful of his famous, brilliantly talented, handsome, rich (and Jewish) older colleague. The roots of Wagner's notorious anti-Semitism can be found partly in this tense relationship.

Wagner was himself born in Leipzig, and studied at the university there. When Mendelssohn became the Leipzig Gewandhaus Kapellmeister in 1835 (then, as now, one of the top jobs in German musical life), Wagner was stuck in the provinces, as a conductor at the Magdeburg opera house. But of course he hoped that Mendelssohn would help to advance his career. On 11 April 1836, he sent a sycophantic letter to Mendelssohn, along with a score of his own immature and derivative Symphony in C major. Mendelssohn never replied to the letter or performed the work, presumably because he could find nothing good to say about the symphony. His silence clearly rankled Wagner for the rest of his life, and in the late 1870s Wagner (by then the most famous living composer) invented the absurd myth that Mendelssohn had hidden or destroyed the score because he was envious of Wagner's talent (and, like many of Wagner's inventions, this one was widely accepted for decades).

Wagner spent most of the 1840s in Dresden, and it was there that he wrote his opera *Lohengrin*. He started the composition in 1846, and it was premiered in Weimar in 1850, under the baton of Franz Liszt. The Bridal Chorus comes near the start of the third and final act, and has the following text:

> Treulich geführt ziehet dahin,
> wo euch der Segen der Liebe bewahr'!
> Siegreicher Mut, Minnegewinn
> eint euch in Treue zum seligsten Paar.
> Streiter der Tugend, schreite voran!
> Zierde der Jugend, schreite voran!
> Rauschen des Festes seid nun entronnen,
> Wonne des Herzens sei euch gewonnen!
> Duftender Raum, zur Liebe geschmückt,
> nehm' euch nun auf, dem Glanze entrückt.
> Treulich geführt ziehet nun ein,
> wo euch der Segen der Liebe bewahr'!
> Siegreicher Mut, Minne so rein
> eint euch in Treue zum seligsten Paar.
>
> (Faithfully guided, draw near
> to where the blessing of love shall preserve you!

Triumphant courage, the reward of love,
joins you in faith as the happiest of couples!
Champion of virtue, proceed!
Jewel of youth, proceed!
Flee now the splendour of the wedding feast,
may the delights of the heart be yours!
This sweet-smelling room, decked for love,
now takes you in, away from the splendour.
Faithfully guided, draw now near
to where the blessing of love shall preserve you!
Triumphant courage, love so pure,
joins you in faith as the happiest of couples!)

In English it is usually sung as 'Here comes the bride, dressed all in white' or indeed 'Here comes the bride, short, fat and wide'. Whereas Mendelssohn's march celebrates the joyously desired (and presumably successful) double wedding of Shakespeare's four lovers, Wagner's music has a much darker undertone. A fatal sword fight is about to take place. The marriage of Elsa and Lohengrin will never be consummated, and by the end of the opera Lohengrin will disappear into the distance on a dove-powered boat as Elsa falls lifeless to the ground.

They are, of course, both terrific pieces of music, and it is quite justified that they are so famous. After all, they are by two of the greatest composers ever. The Mendelssohn conveys a great deal of joy and is an uplifting piece. The Wagner, by contrast, is quite restrained and has an undertone of menace. It has an almost hesitant quality, as if everyone is wondering whether this marriage is really going to work out. Mendelssohn is better at conveying joy than Wagner, who tends to flourish in situations of angst/fear/desire/mystery. In sum, though, posterity has made an excellent choice in keeping these two.

BRIDES, BABES AND BREASTFEEDING

IN these topsy-turvy times, it is not unusual to have reproduced *in advance* of receiving a marriage proposal. If you are following the shotgun model of matrimony, and hurriedly attempting legal union before the offspring emerges, then it is as well to choose your dress wisely. Since so many people wear variations on white nowadays, in spite of none of them being virgins, doing so with a pregnant bump is acceptable (though expect to receive a few sniggers as you lurch up the aisle). Do *not* go empire line in this instance: you will just look mountainous. There is nothing like volumes of snowy satin to put the wedding guest directly in mind of Mont Blanc, forcing them to curb an instinct to prepare oxtail soup and a sturdy carabiner, rather than simply focusing on your radiance. Fitted lace sculpts the contours snugly, and somehow doesn't look so accidental. Mind to book in a fitting the day before the wedding, though: it is hard to anticipate quite the proportions to which you will swell (particularly in the ribcage area), and you (inconveniently) still need to be able to breathe.

If babe is already out and suckling, your dress will need some sort of clever quick-release mechanism. A concealed side zip should be sufficient to allow you to ping yourself out without assistance. Cloakrooms are good places for sneaking off for a quick tipple (of the milk variety only, of course), and if someone walks in on you, yes it *is* undignified — but what can you do? It's normally someone naughty anyway, like a pickpocket, so just leap up and accuse them of stealing. That should take their mind off your engorged appendages. And for heaven's sake, don't get so caught up in a conversation with your mum's friend from work that you forget to feed the mewling infant: you can't risk accruing a big wet patch across your chest (particularly when wedged into something as unforgiving as satin).

How succinctly that cuddly little dependant represents the loving union of husband and wife, in fleshly form. Blah blah blah. Upon finding yourself in the position of Breastfeeding Bride, ensure that you have allowed at least six months from the birth to the Big Day (though whether or not it can still feel as momentous following that particular adventure is contestable). This should permit your body to heal and re-form well enough for you to conceive of its being scrutinized by many, the crushed hips and pulverized lower back able to tolerate high heels, etc. It will also enable your insane, sleep-deprived mind to navigate the emotional and practical demands of organizing a social event of this scale. Rest assured that, other than having the milk bottles strapped to your chest, you will at least not be required to provide any sort of childcare on the day itself. However, you may have some ruffled feathers to smooth following the event, should neither grandmother feel they have been permitted to show off the baby sufficiently to respective gathered acquaintances. Eek. Think of such troubles as a preparatory window on to the realities of a marriage that will be spent managing two wider families and their idiosyncratic array of colourful demands. The Happiest of Times.

HOW TO LOOK FABULOUS IN PHOTOGRAPHS

Do... turn slightly towards the camera with your 'good' side, which tends to be whichever side your hair is parted. Lower the shoulder nearest the camera a little to make your neck look longer; also, standing at an angle makes you look thinner, if you care about such things.

Don't... concentrate so hard on perfecting the above stance that you end up with dead eyes. Try to emanate a bit of sparkle.

Do... stick your chin out to avoid any possibility of a double chin and up to avoid casting shadows.

Don't... laugh, grin too broadly or show too many teeth. Instead, work on looking as though you have just remembered something amusing: a sort of knowing smirk often works rather better than a full-on grin, however chuffed and joyful you may be feeling inside, because it minimizes the appearance of wrinkles and does not show too many teeth, which somehow is never quite elegant. Do, however, be mindful not to offer exactly the same expression in every photograph in existence, a technique pioneered by Victoria Beckham: it just comes across as vain and contrived, as though you are trying just that little bit too hard.

An insoluble dilemma exists when it comes to make-up. The more blusher, eye-liner and lip gloss you wear (within reason) for the Big Day, the better you will look in photographs for evermore and all posterity; the worse, however, you will look on the day, in real life. So it depends which you care about more, which may take some existential soul-searching to decide.

BRITISH ROYAL WEDDINGS OF THE PAST 100 YEARS

Date of wedding	Royal		Intended		Place of wedding
	Initial moniker	Later moniker	Initial moniker	Later moniker	
27 February 1919	HRH Princess Patricia of Connaught	Lady Patricia Ramsey	Captain Alexander Ramsey	Admiral Alexander Ramsey	Westminster Abbey
28 February 1922	HRH Princess Mary	HRH Mary, Princess Royal and Countess of Harewood	The Right Honourable Viscount Lascelles	The Right Honourable The Earl of Harewood	Westminster Abbey
26 April 1923	HRH Prince Albert, Duke of York	King George VI	Lady Elizabeth Bowes-Lyon	HRH The Duchess of York, later The Queen Consort, later HM Queen Elizabeth The Queen Mother	Westminster Abbey
29 November 1934	HRH Prince George	HRH Prince George, Duke of Kent	Princess Marina of Greece and Denmark[1]	HRH The Duchess of Kent	Westminster Abbey
20 November 1947	HRH The Princess Elizabeth	HM The Queen	Lieutenant Philip Mountbatten	HRH The Prince Philip, The Duke of Edinburgh	Westminster Abbey
6 May 1960	HRH The Princess Margaret	HRH Princess Margaret, Countess of Snowdon	Antony Armstrong-Jones	Earl of Snowdon	Westminster Abbey

1   The last princess born abroad to marry into the British royal family.

Date of wedding	Royal		Intended		Place of wedding
	Initial moniker	Later moniker	Initial moniker	Later moniker	
24 April 1963	HRH Princess Alexandra of Kent	HRH Princess Alexandra, The Honourable Lady Ogilvy	The Hon. Angus Ogilvy	The Right Honourable Sir Angus Ogilvy	Westminster Abbey
14 November 1973	HRH Princess Anne	HRH The Princess Royal	Lieutenant Mark Phillips	Captain Mark Phillips	Westminster Abbey
29 July 1981	HRH Prince Charles	HRH The Prince of Wales, Duke of Cornwall	Lady Diana Spencer	Diana, Princess of Wales	St Paul's Cathedral
23 July 1986	HRH Prince Andrew	HRH The Duke of York	Miss Sarah Ferguson	Sarah, Duchess of York	Westminster Abbey
12 December 1992	HRH Princess Anne	HRH The Princess Royal	Captain Timothy Laurence	Vice-Admiral Sir Timothy Laurence	Crathie Kirk
19 June 1999	HRH Prince Edward	HRH The Earl of Wessex	Miss Sophie Rhys-Jones	HRH The Countess of Wessex	St George's Chapel, Windsor Castle
9 April 2005	HRH Prince Charles	HRH The Prince of Wales, Duke of Cornwall	Mrs Camilla Parker-Bowles (née Shand)	HRH The Duchess of Cornwall	Windsor Guildhall
17 May 2008	Peter Phillips	Peter Phillips	Miss Autumn Kelly	Mrs Peter Phillips	St George's Chapel, Windsor Castle
29 April 2011	HRH Prince William of Wales	HRH The Duke of Cambridge	Miss Catherine Middleton	HRH The Duchess of Cambridge	Westminster Abbey
30 July 2011	Zara Phillips	Mrs Mike Tindall	Mr Mike Tindall	Mr Mike Tindall	Canongate Kirk

THE PERFECT *PLACEMENT*

THE *placement* (that is, where everybody sits) at one's wedding reception (such a naff word: couldn't we re-brand it? The old-fashioned 'wedding breakfast' is better, albeit a bit misleading; 'wedding party' is best, though) is one of the primary predictors of the success or otherwise of this most emotionally laden of celebrations. It is the only element of the entire rigmarole that actually matters, other than a) ensuring there is enough food and alcohol and b) playing music that gets people of all ages dancing. Sadly, nobody other than your mum and your best friend will remember the stylishly mismatched vintage jugs on the tables or the über-carefully chosen flowers in the church. What guests will remember is a happy, joyful, brilliant knees-up that celebrates you and your man in every way possible. In all honesty, a wedding reception is only a wedding reception if someone has sex in the bushes and someone is sick in the loo (ideally not the bride, though, in either instance). A *placement* is very helpful in facilitating a range of unexpected connections where your cousin hits it off with your boss and your brother flirts outrageously with your yoga teacher. So although the *placement* is a peculiarly hellish task and can take days and days to complete, it really is worth spending some time over it and giving it some genuine thought. Here are a few additional tips:

Do . . . consider long farmhouse-style tables. They are not the norm at weddings, unfathomably, because they most certainly should be, since the genius of this layout is that it offers guests the opportunity to converse with three people rather than just being stuck with two. It also has the effect of encouraging lively group conversations, which tend to be rather less intense in their nature than the 'So, what do you do?'s of a tête-à-tête.

Don't... flout the diktat that the bride sits next to the groom and is surrounded by immediate family. It may seem boring indeed, since you will almost certainly have spent an awful lot of time with those very people in recent days. But at least it is a chance to eat something, drink something and put the small talk on 'pause' for a while. Phew.

Do... remember that guests *must* be arranged in a 'boy, girl, boy, girl' formation — otherwise the world as we know it might collapse.

Don't... split up couples. Do not seat them next to each other (uncouth); do seat them on the same table (couth).

Do... take the time to consider which of your friends — and everyone has a friend like this — has the admirable ability to talk to anyone, no matter how eccentric, difficult or un-PC they are. These are the people to seat next to your mildly Aspergers-y boss or your embarrassingly unreconstructed grandfather, in the knowledge that they will not rest until they find some way to engage said guest in polite, even stimulating, conversation. After all, everyone is interesting if you prod them hard enough: take the case of the gentleman at one wedding who early on in the evening made it clear to this fair lady author that his one and only topic of conversation was his job at a major credit card company, yet just as she was about to collapse face first into her soup with boredom, he revealed that he was currently responsible for the introduction of credit cards to Africa, and then for the rest of the evening proceeded to fascinate her with various riveting tales of the challenges he faced in this regard. A lesson was most certainly learnt, and not by him.

Don't . . . force any of your friends or family to sit in between two lawyers. Trust me: no one will thank you. Similarly, two recent divorcees are not a fun sandwich, unless the guest in question has a particularly advanced and dark sense of humour.

Do . . . consider themed tables: new parents, singles, etc. On the other hand, do also accept that, with any *placement*, you will always end up with one table of random and mismatched guests. Hey, nobody's perfect, as a great man once said.

Don't . . . be afraid to instruct your male guests to move two seats to their right before pudding, a practice that in recent years has rather fallen out of fashion. This may be because it is rather hard to orchestrate when a large number of people are involved, and it will always annoy those whose flirting is going well and who are already planning their sexy-sex escape. On the other hand, it will thrill those who have exhausted all possible avenues of conversation already, and rescue them from a desultory last half-hour before speeches, with eternal gratitude the result.

With all the expertise you will now have acquired whilst toiling away to get your *placement* just right, consider putting it to good use by instituting a *placement* at all the newly-wed dinner parties you go on to throw. It is the very height of chic, and appreciated so much by guests, however small the gathering.

WHAT TO DO IF A SWARM OF BEES ATTACKS YOUR WEDDING

WHILST in the UK it is rare for a swarm of bees to attack, it does happen if a beehive is accidentally disturbed and the inhabitants fear their nest is in danger. So it is best to be prepared.

- Run. Fast. Bees cannot fly at more than 10mph, so try to outpace them (this is easier said than done in a wedding dress).
- Cover your face to reduce the chances of being stung there. Keep your mouth closed to prevent the bees flying inside.
- It is a myth that you should find a body of water to jump into. The bees will just wait until you come up for air. Bees don't give up easily.
- Most importantly: *get indoors as quickly as possible*. A building or even a car will do. If a few bees come with you, don't panic: they will be less of a threat than the thousands you have just escaped.
- Identify all the places you have been stung in, and then remove all the stingers as quickly as possible in order to reduce the amount of venom that enters your body.
- Call 999.

THE FIRST DANCE

SOMETHING slushy from a film starring Richard Gere or Tom Cruise? A public clinch to the Euro Smash of the summer you got engaged? A professionally choreographed routine that will never live up to the *Dirty Dancing* couple who started this trend?[1] The options are many and the stakes are high. There are some definite no-nos:

- Inviting people to gape at some sort of private and excruciating love-in is no fun for anyone (least of all one's cringing parents). Avoid songs that may give rise to such behaviour. These range from intense student numbers like those of Massive Attack through to the likes of Marvin Gaye's 'Let's Get It On' or 'Sexual Healing'. Any such will set teeth on edge and imaginations involuntarily reeling. Be kind.
- On that note, nothing overtly sexual – particularly if there are children present. Horrid when one sees the poor blighters innocently bopping along. Or one's unwitting parents. So no Madonna or Prince. Even tracks that do not sound racy inevitably harbour the odd atmospheric groan or lewd suggestion. Shudder. Avoid sexy-sex dancing. Desperately uncomfortable. Get a room.
- Avoid melancholia. Nick Drake or Jeff Buckley. It might be beautiful, but boy, it's bleak.
- Nothing too girly (the schmaltzy bit from *Top Gun*, or Joe Cocker and Jennifer Warnes's 'Up Where We Belong', say).

---

1   Search YouTube for 'Dirty Dancing wedding dance' if you haven't already seen this brilliant, hilarious effort from 2005 by British newly-weds Julia and James.

Likewise for saccharine, as with the Carpenters' 'Close to You'. Allow him *some* shred of masculinity.

- If one performs something very rehearsed and tight, such as a choreographed 'Single Ladies' (although clearly, he *has* now 'put a ring on it') or 'Thriller', or whatever, don't look too po-faced. This is meant to be a fun occasion, and you do not wish guests to feel that, if you messed up, your day might be ruined. Nonchalance (even if feigned) is imperative.

And some tips for lessening the pain:

- Invite one's friends to join one sharpish on the floor. This can be prearranged.
- Ask one's DJ for tips: what has worked before, and what definitely has not.
- Look online for home video examples of What Not To Do. That which sounds fun in theory could look disastrous in practice, and one does not want to end up the object of the ridicule of the Western world. Or maybe one does. And that is one's own business. In which case, assiduously ignore everything written here, as it is this pocket book's utmost intention to avoid this incomprehensible possibility.
- Avoid anything too exerting: chances are, however your dress is secured, a bit of luck is playing its part. The risk of exposing the lace confection that's meant for later should *never* be underestimated.

Consider select Dusty Springfield hits (such as 'I Only Want to Be with You': bouncy but clean); the less heartbreaking works of Burt Bacharach are also suitably generation-spanning ('What the World Needs Now Is Love' is ideal). These all have the advantage of floating above the nitty-gritties of a specific and sordid love life, instead embracing more stylized, less graphic themes. And — hear us out — have you thought about something from a Disney animation? Some pre-90s ones are a bit silly (so perfect for putting guests at ease), yet often rather lovely. As with Carly Simon's 'Shoulder to Shoulder' (from the 'acclaimed' *Best of Poo and Heffalump Too*). And the fabulous Pearl Bailey's rendition of 'The Best of Friends' of *The Fox and the Hound* fame. Or why not keep things disco-centric with Justin Timberlake's 'Rock Your Body', or something from the Scissor Sisters' catalogue? Instead of subjugating one's guests to intimate visions of oneself and beloved, choose to reinforce the reality that they are, after all, at a *party*.

The key is: whatever one decides, perform with confidence! If it goes wrong, a wink and a grin help one to own the error in a charming and masterly fashion. This applies in most cases — from falling over, ripped fabric and/or bodily exposure, to the playing of the wrong music, liquid spillage and actual bone breakage.

LET THEM EAT (WEDDING) CAKE

ONCE upon a time, cakes did not differ that much from regular bread. They were just a different shape — rounder, flatter — and contained a little bit of added deliciousness in the form of honey, eggs and/or a fat of some sort; they were more like what we would now call a pie. Popular at weddings was a creation known as 'bride's pye' (there used to be such a thing as 'groom's pye' too), and below is the earliest printed recipe, taken from Robert May's *The Accomplish't Cook* (1665). It was an exceedingly eccentric, elaborate enterprise, and it is surely doubtful that any cook was ever actually brave enough to make it.

ROBERT MAY'S BRIDE'S PYE (1665)

To make an extraordinary Pie, or a Bride Pye of several Compounds, being several distinct Pies on one bottom.

Provide cock-stones and combs, or lamb-stones, and sweet-breads of veal, a little set in hot water and cut to pieces; also two or three ox-pallats blanch't and slic't, a pint of oysters, slic't dates, a handful of pine kernels, a little quantity of broom buds, pickled, some fine interlarded bacon slic't; nine or ten chesnuts rosted and blancht; season them with salt, nutmeg, and some large mace, and close it up with some butter. For the caudle, beat up some butter, with three yolks of eggs, some white or claret 235 wine, the juyce of a lemon or two; cut up the lid, and pour on the lear, shaking it well together; then lay on the meat, slic't lemon, and pickled barberries, and cover it again, let these ingredients be put in the moddle or scollops of the Pye.

Several other Pies belong to the first form, but you must be sure to make the three fashions proportionably answering one the other; you may set them on one bottom of paste, which will be more convenient; or if you set them several you may bake the middle one full of flour, it being bak't and cold, take out the flour in the bottom, & put in live birds, or a snake, which will seem strange to the beholders, which cut up the pie at the Table. This is only for a Wedding to pass away the time.[1]

Now for the other pies you may fill them with several ingredients, as in one you may put oysters, being parboild and bearded, season them with large mace, pepper, some beaten ginger, and salt, season them lightly and fill the Pie, then lay on marrow & some good butter, close it up and bake it. Then make a lear for it with white wine, the oyster liquor, three or four oysters bruised in pieces to make it stronger, but take out the pieces, and an onion, or rub the bottom of the dish with a clove of garlick; it being boil'd, put in a piece of butter, with a lemon, sweet herbs will be good boil'd in it, bound up fast together, cut up the lid, or make a hole to let the lear in, &c.

---

1   It certainly will 'pass away the time' when that snake gets out . . .

Another you may make of prawns and cockles, being seasoned as the first, but no marrow: a few pickled mushrooms (if you have them), it being baked, beat up a piece of butter, a little vinegar, a slic't nutmeg, and the juyce of two or three oranges thick, and pour it into the Pye.

A third you may make a Bird pie; take young Birds, as larks pull'd and drawn, and a forced meat to put in the 236 bellies made of grated bread, sweet herbs minced very small, beef-suet, or marrow minced, almonds beat with a little cream to keep them from oyling, a little parmisan (or none) or old cheese; season this meat with nutmeg, ginger, and salt, then mix them together, with cream and eggs like a pudding, stuff the larks with it, then season the larks with nutmeg, pepper, and salt, and lay them in the pie, put in some butter, and scatter between them pine-kernels, yolks of eggs and sweet herbs, the herbs and eggs being minced very small; being baked make a lear with the juyce of oranges and butter beat up thick, and shaken well together.

For another of the Pies, you may boil artichocks, and take only the bottoms for the Pie, cut them into quarters or less, and season them with nutmeg. Thus with several ingredients you may fill your other Pies.

For the outmost Pies they must be Egg-Pies.

Boil twenty eggs and mince them very small, being blanched, with twice the weight of them of beef-suet fine minced also; then have half a pound of dates slic't with a pound of raisins, and a pound of currans well washed and dryed, and half an ounce of cinamon fine beaten, and a little cloves and mace fine beaten, sugar a quarter of a pound, a little salt, a quarter of a pint of rose-water, and as much verjuyce, and stir and mingle all well together, and fill the pies, and close them, and bake them, they will not be above two hours a baking, and serve them all seventeen upon one dish, or plate, and ice them, or scrape sugar on them; every one of these Pies should have a tuft of paste jagged on the top.

In the sixteenth century, imported sugar became relatively easily available for the first time. The more refined the sugar, the whiter its appearance, and as a result a wedding cake covered with whiter-than-white icing soon became the ultimate status symbol. 'Look how rich my parents are,' it screamed to the assembled guests, particularly if the cake had multiple layers.

By the eighteenth century, cakes looked more as they do today. Eggs had largely replaced yeast as the most popular method for making them rise (or 'leavening', in technical parlance), though this was hideously labour-intensive, since the eggs had to be beaten for hours and hours and hours in order to trap enough air bubbles inside the mixture to give the cake the necessary lightness once baked. Even Mrs Beeton's recipe for a bride cake, from her *Book of Household Management* (1861), required at least half an hour of continual beating.

MRS BEETON'S BRIDE CAKE (1861)

INGREDIENTS: 5 lbs. of the finest flour, 3 lbs. of fresh butter, 5 lbs. of currants, 2 lbs. of sifted loaf sugar, 2 nutmegs, 1/4 oz. of mace, half 1/4 oz. of cloves, 16 eggs, 1 lb. of sweet almonds, 1/2 lb. of candied citron, 1/2 lb. each of candied orange and lemon peel, 1 gill of wine, 1 gill of brandy.

MODE: Let the flour be as fine as possible, and well dried and sifted; the currants washed, picked, and dried before the fire; the sugar well pounded and sifted; the nutmegs grated, the spices pounded; the eggs thoroughly whisked, whites and yolks separately; the almonds pounded with a little orange-flower water, and the candied peel cut in neat slices. When all these ingredients are prepared, mix them in the following manner. Begin working the butter with the hand till it becomes of a cream-like consistency; stir in the sugar, and when the whites of the eggs are whisked to a solid froth, mix them with the butter and sugar; next, well beat up the yolks for 10 minutes, and, adding them to the flour, nutmegs, mace, and cloves, continue beating the whole together for 1/2 hour or longer, till wanted for the oven. Then mix in lightly the currants, almonds, and candied peel with the wine and brandy; and having lined a hoop with buttered paper, fill it with the mixture, and bake the cake in a tolerably quick oven, taking care, however, not to burn it: to prevent this, the top of it may be covered with a sheet of paper. To ascertain whether the cake is done, plunge a clean knife into the middle of it, withdraw it directly, and if the blade is not sticky, and looks bright, the cake is sufficiently baked. These cakes are usually spread with a thick layer of almond icing, and over that another layer of sugar icing, and afterwards ornamented. In baking a large cake like this, great attention must be paid to the heat of the oven; it should not be too fierce, but have a good soaking heat.

Time. 5 to 6 hours.

Average cost. 2s. per lb.

It was only with the invention of chemical raising agents like bicarbonate of soda and baking powder in the late nineteenth century that the cake-making process became a little less laborious.

Because one can never have too much information about cakes, let us now move on to the science of these wondrous creations. What is the magic that turns this gloopy mixture into a sight so sweet to behold? In a word: heat. The moment the cake mixture is placed in the oven, the solid fats in it begin to melt, releasing much of the air and water trapped within them. The air expands, which increases the volume of the cake and helps it rise, while the water evaporates into steam, which performs a similar function. And, in other gas-related news, the heat not only helps activate the raising agent but also speeds up the rate of fermentation, and therefore the rate at which carbon dioxide is released.

Another effect of the fats melting is that they coat all the starches, egg proteins and gluten strands contained within the cake mixture, thereby tenderizing them. In other words, the more fat, the tenderer the cake – yum. The fats also help thin out the batter or dough, though if they thin out too much, the structure of the cake collapses. However, once the temperature of the oven reaches about 65°C, the heat causes gluten and egg protein to dry out and subsequently stiffen – in other words, transform from liquid to solid – and thus create the structure that constitutes the final size and shape of the all-hallowed baked creation. Starch helps, too.

And that is how a cake is made. But, oh, how life's trials and tribulations never end, for now comes the next sleep-stealing conundrum: what *sort* of cake to have, by Jove? An old-fashioned tiered wedding cake has become the height of vulgarity, and anyway, why succumb to convention when there are so many other fabulous options? One suspects that not a few sweet-toothed women have planned a wedding solely for the sake of the cake-tasting sessions. On the next page is a reminder of some of the different types of cakes one could choose. Some would be a more eccentric choice than others – there is probably a good reason why one has never seen a Bakewell tart served at a wedding before – but so be it: who doesn't want to spend more time thinking about cake? And anyone who doesn't may be considered a traitor to womankind.

Angel cake	Three layers of sponge – pink, yellow and white – topped with a layer of cream or icing, and cut into long thin slices. The naffest of naff choices and therefore rather characterful, perversely.
Apple cake	Big in the West Country, often with added cinnamon and nutmeg.
Bakewell tart	Frangipane – a sponge-like filling made with ground almonds – contained within a shortcrust pastry case that has been spread with jam. To some a delicacy, to others their worst nightmare. Originally from Derbyshire.
Banana cake	Unbelievably easy to make and almost always universally appreciated. A homely cake.
Banoffee pie	Rather fiddly, especially for those who choose the boiling-cans-of-condensed-milk-for-four-hours route (not recommended, and you can now buy jars of dulce de leche in the supermarket) but totally worth the effort. What sort of madman does not like a banana/toffee combo? Though it can be a bit reminiscent of T.G.I. Friday's . . .
Bara brith	Welsh name that means 'speckled bread'. Distinguishing feature: dried fruit.
Battenberg	Half the cake mixture is dyed yellow, and the other half is dyed pink, then each sponge is cut into two long thin cuboids and stuck together with jam, ideally of the apricot persuasion. Hence when cut in half, the cake displays a distinctive four-squared pattern that reminds many of us of tea with our grandmothers. The story goes that this cake was invented in honour of the wedding of Prince Louis of Battenberg to Queen Victoria's granddaughter, Princess Victoria, each of the four squares symbolizing one of the four Battenberg princes. Like many suspiciously neat historical explanations of this sort, however, it might be true, but it very well also might not.
Black Forest gateau	Known in Germany, its land of origin, as Schwarzwälder Kirschtorte. The crucial ingredient is Schwarzwälder Kirschwasser, a cherry liqueur from the Black Forest area of south-west Germany. Layers of chocolate cake sandwiched together with cherries and whipped cream and decorated on top with the same.
Carrot cake	Mmmm, perfect. Makes you feel vaguely healthy, but you still get to eat cake. Especially good with cream cheese icing.

Cheesecake	A biscuity crust topped with a cheese-based filling and then a fruit compote of some kind, most commonly strawberry, raspberry, blackcurrant, or lemon curd. No baking required. Popular as far back as ancient Greece; the Greek physician Aegimus wrote a whole book on the subject. In Britain a mixture of cream cheese, cream and sugar is common but the filling differs around the world: the Italians prefer ricotta cheese, the Germans, Dutch and Poles tend to side with quark. Considered by some to be a bit too desserty to work well in the context of a wedding.
Chocolate brownies	Comparable to bad sex: a bad brownie is still better than no brownie at all. A big stack of them cut into bite-size pieces, scattered with a few fresh raspberries and some icing sugar, is excellent for large groups.
Chocolate cake	Can't go wrong. It's chocolate in a cake. Also consider chocolate fudge cake, the humble chocolate cake's vastly superior cousin. Ridiculously delicious with ice cream.
Christmas cake	An eccentric choice, unless you're getting married in the week of this other Big Day.
Coffee and walnut cake	The appeal of this is hard to comprehend: one would always rather just have a coffee and some nuts, surely. However, this is perhaps a minority stance to take, especially amongst the older generation.
Cupcake (also known as fairy cake)	A teeny-tiny cake originally baked in individual pottery cups — hence the original name — and now appropriated by the Americans. In Britain it acquired the more whimsical name of 'fairy cake', and here fairy cakes tend to be smaller and less elaborately decorated. Very chic about three years ago, but now the choice only of someone who has been watching too many *Sex and the City* re-runs.
Fruit cake	The standby of old ladies, with good reason: it lasts *forever* in a tin.
Ginger cake	Somehow, this never tastes as good as the shop-bought Jamaica Ginger Cake one remembers from the 1970s. Easy to make, though, and massively improved by the use of fresh ginger.
Ice-cream cake	Underrated. Ice cream in the shape of a cake. What's not to like?
Lemon drizzle cake	The housewife's favourite. Always good with tea, especially for some reason if one is already feeling a bit stuffed.
Madeira cake	The cake Celia Johnson probably would have eaten at the station in *Brief Encounter*. A lovely buttery, lemony cake, very easy to make and delicious in its simplicity.

Marble cake	Two bowls of vanilla cake mixture, one with added chocolate, are blended together to form a cake that's streaky in appearance, a bit like bad highlights in your hair.
Millefeuille	Three thin layers of puff pastry alternated with two layers of pastry cream, whipped cream or jam, with a sprinkling of icing sugar or cocoa on top. Originally from France (the name translates as 'thousand-leaf', a reference to its many layers of pastry), in Britain it is also known as a 'custard slice'.
Parkin	Parkin is a Yorkshire delicacy: it is a sort of gingerbread with added treacle and porridge. To serve fresh parkin is to be guilty of a major faux pas. Rather, it must be allowed to age for a week or two before one even thinks about eating it.
Sachertorte	Two layers of bitter chocolate sponge cake sandwiched together with apricot jam and covered with dark chocolate icing. Often served with a side of whipped cream. Delia Smith has a great recipe. Invented in 1832 for the Austrian statesman Prince Wenzel von Metternich by a sixteen-year-old apprentice chef named Franz Sacher, but only popularized much later when Sacher's son Eduard opened the Hotel Sacher in Vienna in 1876, where it was served as the speciality dessert.
Swiss roll	A bold choice for a wedding indeed. Flour, sugar and eggs are mixed together and baked in a sheet pan. The resulting rectangular, thin, flat cake is then spread with jam or cream, rolled up and cut up into round slices.
Tarte tatin	Probably invented and certainly popularized in the 1880s by sisters Caroline and Stéphanie Tatin, proprietors of the Hotel Tatin in Lamotte-Beucron, a town about 100 miles south of Paris. It is essential to use a variety of apple that holds its shape when cooked like Granny Smiths or Golden Delicious; otherwise one just ends up with a mess of apple sauce.
Tiramisu	The Italian name means 'pick me up' in English. *Savoiardi* biscuits are soaked in coffee and then placed in alternate layers with a mixture of mascarpone cheese, sugar and eggs flavoured with cocoa powder and Marsala wine.
Victoria sponge cake	Inspired by Queen Victoria, as so much was, this is a simple cake made of flour, sugar, eggs and baking powder, sandwiched together with raspberry jam and topped with a sprinkling of icing sugar. A classic. Glam it up with whipped cream and fresh fruit (strawberries, raspberries) added to the jam in the middle.

HOW TO WALTZ

CONSIDER attempting to master the waltz in the weeks before your wedding. Not only is it a useful life skill generally, but it is also helpful to be able to hit the dance floor once or twice with the older generation, even if it is to a modern song written in triple time such as 'Rainbow Connection', 'Norwegian Wood', 'I Put a Spell on You', 'Moon River', 'What's New Pussycat' or 'Piano Man', or a few brilliant ones by Elliot Smith that you may or may not decide are appropriate in the context of a wedding. The specific steps for a waltz are best learnt from a YouTube video; however, additional guidance may be found in a book written in 1816 by Thomas Wilson, the dancing master at the King's Theatre, Opera House, of the Theatres Royal, Drury Lane and Covent Garden. His book *A Description of the Correct Method of Waltzing* was the first detailed English-language description of the waltz as it was danced when it first came to England during the Regency period. Here are a few of the sage pieces of advice Wilson offers:

It is almost useless to mention, that if the Lady and Gentleman who are partners are not of an equal height in stature, or nearly so, great difficulty will arise in the performance of the attitudes, and will consequently produce an appearance of extreme awkwardness.

To learners, it very frequently occurs, that for want of practice in dancing, they do not possess sufficient balance, to enable them to perform the several movements with that ease which is absolutely necessary to the production of the required effect in waltzing;

and, consequently, in order to obtain support from their partners in the performance of it, are generally guilty of so gross an impropriety, as actually to pull their partners round the room — such is not waltzing.

Learners must necessarily endeavour to acquire a feeling of what they are performing, as they will be thereby soon enabled, on paying a proper attention to the subject (on the contrary of hanging with great weight on their partners) to obtain a balance, so as to perform all the several movements in succession, as described for the feet, arms, &c., with an ease and confidence, that never fails in affording much comfortable pleasure to the dancers; and, to the lookers-on, a spectacle of graceful beauty.

A little practice will also be necessary for learners of waltzing, previous to their being able to enjoy a long continuance of it; as they generally, at first, experience a giddiness, occasioned by the closely repeated and continued turnings. This affection wears off most frequently after a few days practice.

It is frequently the case with persons in waltzing, to indulge themselves extravagantly, in an improper manner, by throwing the head and body from one Side to the other, in a sallying or swinging Direction.[1] It is much more graceful and decorous also, in performing those steps requiring an accompanying turning of the body, to keep the body in an easy, but yet upright, steady Posture which will assist the more correct performance of the steps, and of the attitudes to be performed at the same time.

Thomas Wilson, *A Description of the Correct Method of Waltzing* (1816)

---

1   A move still seen on many a dance floor even today.

EIGHT ANSWERS TO THE QUESTION 'SO, WHEN WILL WE BE HEARING THE PATTER OF TINY FEET?'

IT seems people feel it is socially acceptable to ask this most personal of questions, when surely they would never ask, 'So, how is your uterus doing today?' Or perhaps they would. Reader, we wish we could provide some clue as to the most likely quarters from which such a downright rude and intimate query might emanate. The sad truth is, this crushingly mood-flattening question could well pop forth from almost any of one's acquaintances. In fact, the less they know about one, the more likely it seems they are to go right ahead and ask.

The following retorts to this oh-so-vulgar of enquiries should certainly serve to shut them up. With any luck, they might also send them scuttling back to Middle England, cheeks a-burning and stomach a-churning. Let's begin gently.

- 'Oh, Rentokil came round and put out some traps before we moved in, so fingers crossed, we'll be OK.' [Jolly grimace.]
- 'Sorry? Patter of . . . ? I don't know what you mean . . .' [The interlocutor will feel so exposed by the blocking of their dependable British metaphors that they may actually end up asking *if you're planning on having children*. Imagine! Far easier to say 'No' to that, and end all further impertinent probing.]
- 'Well, I'm really just keen on making shedloads of cash in my life – illegally, if necessary – and blowing it on male prostitutes and a few guided coach excursions round Britain.' [No physical directions required.]

- 'I despise children.' [Ideally said whilst the quizzer's darling grandfolk are racing around one's legs. A harsh swatting motion in the children's direction will add colour and emphasis.]
- 'Well, we're just a bit too busy to have sex right now.' [Best shrieked at a parental bash, during a lull.]
- 'Oh, didn't you hear? Our bodies can't make love, so . . .' [Ditto. The unforgivable phrase 'make love', when said out loud, has a hilarious effect on a person's complexion.]
- 'I'm infertile. Hopefully!' [Another jolly grimace. The closing expression of desire that this is indeed the case will obstruct the obligatory passing on of details of the interrogator's daughter's fertility specialist, who 'works miracles'.]
- 'Paul's impotent.' [Adapt according to name of husband, obviously, whilst shrugging nonchalantly.]

BRRRRMMMMM BRRRRMMMMM, HONK HONK; OR, TOP TEN CARS IN WHICH TO DEPART FROM A WEDDING

NOT everyone will have the good fortune to have a father who, as heir to the throne, has a long-standing relationship with Aston Martin motor cars, and thus is able to lend you and your new wife his concours-level, immaculate, 1969 DB6 model which he has had knocking around in the garage at the estate for the past forty years. So for the rest of us, the choice of car in which to depart from one's wedding can be somewhat more prosaic. But that does not mean one must feel compelled to fall back on the tried-and-trusted white vintage Rolls-Royce or Daimler (to which, however, it is impossible to hold serious objections: if it is good enough for Mick and Bianca Jagger, it is good enough for anyone). Here are some alternatives.

2012 The Fisker Karma: In white. The rich person's nod to the environment. The billionaires' Prius. This all-electric car sets a buyer back some £100,000 (thereby putting it beyond the reach of most of us), but as cool, eco, contemporary design goes there is nothing better in which to be seen leaving your picturesque Cotswolds wedding reception. Not the best for leg room, of course, but you cannot have everything.

1982 Rolls-Royce Silver Spirit: In brown. Kermit's car from the 2011 *Muppets* film. If ever there was a car that said, 'I like the better things in life but I'm totally broke', then this is that car.

1994 Range Rover: LPG. The eco-friendly farmers' car of choice. Will get you out of any muddy patches encountered on the 'cross-country' drive to your Manor Hotel honeymoon suite.

1976 Daimler Double 6: The gentleman thief's car of choice adds a touch of 1970s gangster chic to the occasion. The car footballers would have bought in the 1970s if they'd been paid as much then as they are today. Worth every penny. Two petrol tanks will ensure that you can arrive at your destination without having to stop off to refuel – no matter how far away you go.

1968 Bug-eyed Sprite: Because it looks funny. And it's not an MG.

1974 Jensen Interceptor: The coolest car ever made. TM.

1972 Citroën DS: For years, this car ferried around French presidents, prime ministers, deputies, mayors, ambassadors. And if it is good enough for them, then it is good enough for you.

1983 Trabant: With its two-strike petrol engine (it has roughly the same power output as your current lawnmower), this will not allow a speedy getaway. But in these parsimonious times you may well be applauded as you leave the wedding reception for your obvious economizing. But of course you know these cars are secretly cool and still very much in use in East Berlin.

Tandem bicycle: Only joking.

Taxi: There is something gloriously *Rita, Sue and Bob Too* about leaving your wedding in a minicab. I am picturing a mid-'80s Ford Granada, but these days no doubt you'll end up in a Toyota Avensis. Never mind: the overall sense of low-end glamour will still be the same. If in town, a black cab is also not a terrible idea: excellent leg room, and therefore easy for the dress. Just remember to take cash. The groom's trouser pocket is probably the best location for it, although you may get a discount if the bride fishes the grubby wedge of used £20 notes from her garter . . .

THE HARASSING BRIDAL TOUR

The young couple walk daily abroad, being entertained and treated by all their friends and acquaintance; and then travell into the Country for their pleasure. If it be true that there is a Mountain of Mirth and pleasure for young married people to ascend unto, these are certainly the finest and smoothest conductors to it; that, because it was impossible to invite every one to the Wedding, this sweet Venus must be led abroad, and shewed to all her husbands friends & acquaintance: yea, all the World must see what a pretty couple they are, and how handsomly they agree together. To which end they trick and prick themselves daily up in their best apparel; garnishing both the whole city and streets with tatling and pratling; & staring into the houses of all their acquaintance to see whether they are looked at.

Aphra Behn, *The Ten Pleasures of Marriage* (1682)

THIS description of the days immediately after a wedding shows the couple visiting friends and relations to announce their newly-wed status to the community. Occasionally just-marrieds would travel abroad, but always accompanied by friends and family. It was not until the early nineteenth century that what used to be known as 'the bridal tour' was renamed 'the honeymoon' and it became more usual for the bride and groom to spend it privately and alone, so that by the 1870s the fashionable advice given by Victorian etiquette books was to avoid the 'harassing bridal tour' in favour of a 'honeymoon of repose, exempted from the claims of society'.

These days, it would not occur to most of us to spend our honeymoon visiting friends and relations, as per Aphra Behn.

You also do not — repeat, *not* — want to race around the country getting stuck in motorway traffic so that you can then jet off on an aeroplane to some far-off 'luxury destination' that advertises itself as being 'the ideal honeymoon spot'. Ugh — how hideously vulgar to have everyone else in the same boat as you; it's as though you are all wearing a sign around your neck proclaiming, 'Hey! I'm having lots of sex!' Of course we all want people to know, but enough can be conveyed with a blissed-out smirk without having to endure a week of wandering around in a flurry of rose petals all the time. One might suspect that any newly-weds who choose to honeymoon in such a destination have gleaned their entire knowledge of romance from rom-coms starring Kate Hudson — which everyone knows are bad, bad, *bad*, for your soul.

Instead, please, please, consider a UK destination for your honeymoon. Cornwall or the Lake District, perhaps, or central Dorset or the Isle of Skye: all are impossibly romantic. Even in the inevitable bad weather there is nowhere more beautiful on earth, especially when all you want to do is stay in bed anyway. Jump on a train, luxuriate in a buffet-car G&T, and enjoy the time to giggle over all the various hilarities of the day before: the embarrassing inappropriateness of what tactless aunt A said to single friend B, the cringeworthy lecherousness of cousin C as he pursued work colleague D. And thus whilst for some their wedding is the happiest day of their life (and it can, of course, be brilliant fun and truly the best party ever), for others it is the day *after* the wedding that really shines: the stress is over and all that's left is you and the love of your life, some beautiful scenery, and as many teeny-tiny bottles of alcohol as you can drink.

LENGTH OF NATIONAL RAILWAY ROUTE AT YEAR END, AND PASSENGER TRAVEL BY NATIONAL RAILWAY AND LONDON UNDERGROUND (1900–2011)

Year	Length of National Rail route (kilometres)[1]			National Rail[2]	
	Total route	Electrified route[3]	Open to passenger traffic	Passenger journeys (million)	Passenger kilometres (billion)
1900	29,783	..	..	..	..
1919	32,420	1,321	..	2,064	..
1923	32,462	1,122	..	1,772	..
1928	32,565	1,901	..	1,250	..
1933	32,345	2,403	..	1,159	..
1938	32,081	3,378	..	1,237	30.6
1946	31,963	..	..	1,266	47.0
1947	31,950	1,455	..	1,140	37.0
1948	31,593	1,455	..	1,024	34.2
1949	31,500	1,489	..	1,021	34.0
1950	31,336	1,489	..	1,010	32.5
1951	31,152	1,487	..	1,030	33.5
1952	31,022	1,508	..	1,017	33.3
1953	30,935	1,508	..	1,015	33.5
1954	30,821	1,577	..	1,020	33.3
1955	30,676	1,577	23,820	994	32.7
1956	30,618	1,624	23,612	1,029	34.0
1957	30,521	1,621	23,532	1,101	36.4
1958	30,333	1,622	23,621	1,090	35.0
1959	29,877	1,799	22,632	1,069	35.8
1960	29,562	2,034	22,314	1,037	34.7

1   The length of route is that managed by Network Rail (formerly Railtrack). It does not include track managed by private companies or Passenger Transport Executive services operating on separately managed track.

2   Franchised operators only.

3   Pre-1947 figures refer to track length, not route length, and include electrified sidings. In 1947 electrified track kilometres totalled 3,370.

| | Length of National Rail route (kilometres)[1] | | | National Rail[2] | |
Year	Total route	Electrified route[3]	Open to passenger traffic	Passenger journeys (million)	Passenger kilometres (billion)
1962	28,117	2,511	20,785	965	31.8
1963*	27,330	2,556	20,328	938	31.5
1964	25,735	2,659	18,781	928	32.0
1965	24,011	2,886	17,516	865	30.1
1966	22,082	3,064	16,359	835	29.7
1967	21,198	3,241	15,904	837	29.1
1968	20,080	3,182	15,242	831	28.7
1969	19,470	3,169	15,088	806	29.6
1970	18,989	3,162	14,637	824	30.4
1971	18,738	3,169	14,484	816	30.1
1972	18,417	3,178	14,499	754	28.3
1973	18,227	3,462	14,375	728	29.8
1974	18,168	3,647	14,373	733	30.9
1975	18,118	3,655	14,431	730	30.3
1976	18,007	3,735	14,407	702	28.6
1977	17,973	3,767	14,413	702	29.3
1978	17,901	3,716	14,396	724	30.7
1979	17,795	3,718	14,100	748	31.1
1980	17,645	3,718	14,394	760	30.3
1981	17,431	3,729	14,394	719	29.7
1982	17,229	3,753	14,371	630	27.2
1983	16,964	3,750	14,375	694	29.5
1984/85	16,816	3,798	14,304	701	29.5
1985/86	16,752	3,809	14,310	686	30.4
1986/87*	16,670	4,156	14,304	738	30.8
1987/88	16,633	4,207	14,302	798	32.4
1988/89	16,599	4,376	14,309	822	34.3
1989/90	16,587	4,546	14,318	812	33.3
1990/91	16,584	4,912	14,317	810	33.2
1991/92	16,588	4,886	14,291	792	32.5
1992/93	16,528	4,910	14,317	770	31.7

	Length of National Rail route (kilometres)[1]			National Rail[2]	
Year	Total route	Electrified route[3]	Open to passenger traffic	Passenger journeys (million)	Passenger kilometres (billion)
1994/95[5]	16,542	4,970	14,359	735	28.7
1995/96	16,666	5,163	15,002	761	30.0
1996/97	16,666	5,176	15,034	801	32.1
1997/98	16,656	5,166	15,024	846	34.7
1998/99	16,659	5,166	15,038	892	36.3
1999/00	16,649	5,167	15,038	931	38.5
2000/01	16,652	5,167	15,042	957	38.2
2001/02	16,652	5,167	15,042	960	39.1
2002/03	16,670	5,167	15,042	976	39.7
2003/04	16,493	5,200	14,883	1,012	40.9
2004/05[4]	16,116	5,200	14,328	1,040	41.7
2005/06	15,810	5,205	14,356	1,076	43.1
2006/07	15,795	5,250	14,353	1,145	46.2
2007/08[4]	15,814	5,250	14,484	1,218	48.9
2008/09	15,814	5,250	14,494	1,266	50.6
2009/10	15,753	5,239	14,482	1,258	51.1
2010/11	15,777	5,262	14,506	1,354	54.1
2011/12	15,742	5,261	14,506	1,462	57.3
2012/13	15,753	5,265	14,504	1,503	58.4

Source: Department for Transport

* On 27 March 1963, the chairman of the British Railways Board, Richard Beeching, published his infamous report *The Reshaping of British Railways*, which recommended closing a third of the country's 7,000 railway stations and cutting passenger train services from over 5,000 miles of track. The government acted upon his advice very quickly, and the result was the destruction of much of Britain's railway system and by extension the beginning of the end for Britain itself. Sort of.

4　Break in series due to a change in methodology.
5　Break in series. From 1994/95 figures include an element of double counting, as a journey involving more than one operator is scored against each operator. This contrasts with former British Rail data for which a through ticket journey was counted only once.

MARRIED LOVE

MARRIED *Love* by Marie Stopes was first published in 1918, just eight months after the end of the First World War and one month after women got the vote (albeit with limitations). It was a momentous time, and Stopes's book was part of it. It was the first book to explain to women the mechanics of sex – how, when, why – and was thus truly revolutionary to a generation who knew little to nothing about such matters.

Marie Stopes was born in 1880. She studied botany at UCL and then Munich University; then she had a stint at Manchester University, where she specialized in the reproductive organs of plants. A miserable affair with a married Japanese botanist led to her rather rashly publishing their love letters – imagine! – and then, in 1911, rushing into marriage with Reginald Ruggles Gate (worth marrying just for the name, surely). A Canadian scientist of genetics, he had proposed within a week of their meeting; 'Except that he has a stupid little nose, he seems absolutely perfect,' Marie wrote to her younger sister Winnie.

The marriage was not a happy one. Just three years later, Marie sought an annulment (the law did not allow women to divorce) on the grounds that the marriage had never been consummated. In court she was forced to answer such hideous questions as 'With regard to your husband's parts, did they ever get rigid at all?' to which she replied, 'On hundreds of occasions on which we had what I thought were relations, I only remember three occasions on which it was partially rigid, and then it was never effectively rigid.' Oh, the humiliation! It was an experience she drew on when writing *Married Love*: 'In my own marriage I paid such a terrible price for sex-ignorance that I feel knowledge gained at such a cost should be placed in the service of humanity.'

Marie was then introduced to Humphrey Roe, a Mancunian who had made a fortune helping run his family's aircraft business. He not only agreed to put up the money to publish *Married Love*; he also fell in love with her. There was a bit of a hitch, in that Humphrey was already engaged to a clergyman's daughter named Ethel Burgess, but a couple of huge, horrible scenes persuaded Ethel to agree that Humphrey could break off the engagement, as long as he promised to wait six months before marrying Marie. Marie was so desperate to marry, however – Humphrey was due at the Front in his new-found role as a lieutenant in the RAF – that they decided to do it in secret at the register office in Hanover Square. The ceremony was followed a few weeks later by a more public church wedding at St Margaret's, Westminster.

The day proved rainy (perhaps Marie consoled herself with the old saying that rain on one's wedding day is good luck), but in all the photographs that exist of the happy day Humphrey, dashingly decked out in his uniform, is gallantly holding an umbrella over his new bride to keep her dry. She, sadly, looks a bit of a fright, in a shapeless, complicated, confusing excuse for a dress: made of cream satin and silver brocade, it fell to an unflattering length, just at the ankles, and was accessorized with a tulle veil fastened to her hair with a wreath of orange blossom and some matching orange blossom at her waist. The entire ensemble was monstrous and appears designed to give a man second thoughts, but in those days it was just what women wore. Fashion was apparently the one arena where Marie did succumb to convention.

Married Love was originally entitled *They Twain*, so thank goodness that was ditched or surely it would have sunk without a trace and we would never have heard of it. The book sold over 2,000 copies in its first fortnight. The most crucial passages are to be found in Chapter V which, considering what is coming up, is rather dryly entitled 'Mutual Adjustment'. Following a bit of information about how the average ejaculation contains 200–500 million sperm – 'Thus by a single ejaculation one man might fertilize nearly all the marriageable women in the world!' she comments, rather alarmingly – she goes on to reveal that 'the timing and the frequency of union are the points about which questions are oftenest asked by the ignorant and well-meaning, and are most misunderstood'. And so she sets out to offer some much-needed information to a generation of men and women for whom sex was a forbidden topic of discussion.

Right. Brace yourself.

What actually happens in an act of union should be known. After the preliminaries have mutually roused the pair, the stimulated penis, enlarged and stiffened, is pressed into the woman's vagina. Ordinarily when a woman is not stimulated, the walls of this canal, as well as the exterior lips of soft tissue surrounding it, are dry and rather crinkled, and the vaginal opening is smaller than the man's extended penis. But when the woman is what is physiologically called tumescent (that is, when she is ready for union and has been profoundly stirred) these parts are flushed by the internal blood supply and to some extent are turgid like those of the man, while a secretion of mucus lubricates the channel of the vagina. In an ardent woman the vagina may even spontaneously open and close. (So powerful is the influence of thought on our bodily structure, that in some people all these physical results may be brought about by the thought of the loved one, by the enjoyment of tender words and kisses, and the beautiful subtleties of wooing.) It can therefore be readily imagined that when the man tries to enter a woman whom he has not wooed to the point of stimulating her natural physical reactions of preparation, he is endeavouring to force his entry through a dry-walled opening too small for it. He may thus cause the woman actual pain, apart from the mental revolt and loathing she is likely to feel for a man who so regardlessly uses her. On the other hand, in the tumescent woman the opening, already naturally expanded, is lubricated by mucus, and all the nerves and muscles are ready to react and easily accept the man's entering organ . . .

When the two have met and united, the usual result is that, after a longer or shorter interval, the man's mental and physical stimulation reaches a climax in sensory intoxication and in the ejaculation of semen. Where the two are perfectly adjusted, the woman simultaneously reaches the crisis of nervous and muscular reactions very similar to his.[1] This mutual orgasm is extremely important, but in many cases the man's climax comes so swiftly that the woman's reactions are not nearly ready, and she is left without it. Though in some instances the woman may have one or more crises before the man achieves his, it is, perhaps, hardly an exaggeration to say that 70 or 80 per cent of our married women (in the middle classes) are deprived of the full orgasm through the excessive speed of the husband's reactions, or through some maladjustment of the relative shapes and positions of the organs. So deep-seated, so profound, are woman's complex sex-instincts as well as her organs, that in rousing them the man is rousing her whole body and soul. And this takes time. More time, indeed, than the average, uninstructed husband gives to it. Yet woman has at the surface a small vestigial organ called the clitoris, which corresponds morphologically to the man's penis, and which, like

---

1 'Crisis' indeed!

it, is extremely sensitive to touch-sensations. This little crest, which lies anteriorly between the inner lips round the vagina, enlarges when the woman is really tumescent, and by the stimulation of movement it is intensely roused and transmits this stimulus to every nerve in her body. But even after a woman's dormant sex-feeling is aroused and all the complex reactions of her being have been set in motion, it may even take as much as from ten to twenty minutes of actual physical union to consummate her feeling, while two or three minutes often completes the union for a man who is ignorant of the need to control his reactions so that both may experience the added benefit of a mutual crisis to love . . .

Marie Stopes, Married Love (1918)

It is a short book, but terribly interesting and important — this sort of stuff had never been described in print before, *ever* — and would make a terrifically unusual wedding present (to yourself?): there are lots of beautiful old editions available on www.abe.com.

I'M COMING; OR, WHAT TO DO IF YOUR NEW HUSBAND HAS A HEART ATTACK ON YOUR WEDDING NIGHT

IN *Private Benjamin* (1980), one of the greatest comedy films ever (it just gets funnier and more innovative on every viewing), Yale Goodman, the new husband of Judy Benjamin (Goldie Hawn), dies of a heart attack in the midst of having sex with her on the night of their wedding. At his funeral, the following exchange occurs:

> MRS GOODMAN (Yale's mother): Please dear, I need to know. What were his last words?
>
> JUDY BENJAMIN: I'm coming.

Funny though this is, a real heart attack is of course no joke. So, best to be prepared. Here is what St John Ambulance (the UK's leading first aid charity) advises in the case of a suspected heart attack:

1. Look for:
   - Persistent central chest pain – often described as vice-like or a heavy crushing pressure
   - Pain spreading (radiating) to the jaw, neck and down one or both arms
   - Breathlessness
   - Discomfort high in the abdomen, similar to indigestion
   - Possible collapse without warning
   - Ashen skin and blueness at the lips

- Rapid, weak pulse which may be irregular
- Profuse sweating, skin cold to the touch
- Gasping for air (air hunger)
- Nausea and/or vomiting.

2. Sit them in the 'W' position, that is, semi-recumbent (sitting up at about 75° to the ground) with knees bent.

3. Call 999/112 for emergency help and tell ambulance control you suspect a heart attack.

4. If available and not allergic, give them a 300mg aspirin tablet to chew slowly (provided they are not under 16 years of age). If they have any medication for angina, such as tablets or a spray, assist them to take it. Constantly monitor and record breathing and pulse rate, until help arrives.

5. If they become unconscious before help arrives, refer to the treatment for someone unconscious but breathing:
   - Turn them on to their side
   - Lift chin forward in open airway position and adjust hand under the cheek as necessary
   - Check they cannot roll forwards or backwards
   - Monitor breathing continuously
   - If injuries allow, turn them to the other side after 30 minutes.

6. If not breathing at any point, administer CPR:
   - Place heel of your hand in the centre of the chest
   - Place other hand on top and interlock fingers
   - Keeping your arms straight and your fingers off the chest, press down by 5–6 centimetres and release the pressure, keeping your hands in place
   - Repeat the compressions 30 times, at a rate of 100–120 per minute (about the speed of the song 'Nelly the Elephant').

* Do not stop unless:

- emergency help arrives and takes over
- they show signs of recovery such as coughing, opening eyes, speaking or moving purposefully and breathing normally
- you become so exhausted that you cannot carry on.

Current advice is to concentrate mainly on the pushing on the chest as detailed above: this is by far the most important element of CPR If you are feeling confident, however, then proceed with the next stage, which is to administer rescue breaths:

- Ensure the airway is open
- Pinch nose firmly closed
- Take a deep breath and seal your lips around their mouth
- Blow into the mouth until the chest rises
- Remove your mouth and allow the chest to fall
- Repeat once more.
- Continue resuscitation, 30 compressions to 2 rescue breaths

* Do not stop unless:

- emergency help arrives and takes over
- they show signs of recovery such as coughing, opening eyes, speaking or moving purposefully and breathing normally
- you become so exhausted that you cannot carry on.

'MY HUSBAND' IN THIRTY-FIVE LANGUAGES

Albanian	*Burri im*
Basque	*Nire senarra*
Catalan	*El meu marit*
Croatian	*Moj suprug*
Czech	*Můj manžel*
Danish	*Min mand*
Dutch	*Mijn man*
Estonian	*Mu abikaasa*
Filipino	*Aking asawa*
Finnish	*Mieheni*
French	*Mon mari*
Galician	*Meu home*
German	*Mein Mann*
Hungarian	*A férjem*
Icelandic	*Maðurinn minn*
Indonesian	*Suami saya*
Irish	*Mo fear céile*
Italian	*Mio marito*
Latin	*Vir meus*
Latvian	*Mans vīrs*
Lithuanian	*Mano vyras*
Malay	*Saya suami*
Maltese	*My raġel*
Norwegian	*Min mann*
Polish	*Mój mąż*
Portuguese	*Meu marido*
Romanian	*Soțul meu*
Slovak	*Môj manžel*
Slovenian	*Moj mož*
Spanish	*Mi marido*
Swahili	*Mume wangu*
Swedish	*Min man*
Turkish	*Kocam*
Vietnamese	*Chồng tôi*
Welsh	*Mae fy ngŵr*

BOOKS ABOUT MARRIAGE PUBLISHED IN BRITAIN BEFORE 1900

Year	Title	Author
1682	*The Ten Pleasures of Marriage, relating all the delights and contentments that are mask'd under the bands of matrimony'*	A. Marsh (the pseudonym of Aphra Behn)
1693	*The Salamanca Wedding; or, A True Account of a Swearing Doctor's marriage with a Muggletonian Widow in Breadstreet*	Thomas Brown
1696	*The Batchelor's Directory: being a treatise of the excellence of marriage, of its necessity, and the means to live happy in it: together with an apology for the women against the calumnies of the men*	Anonymous
1700	*Joy and Happiness to Youth; or, the young men and maidens encouragement to speedy marriage: containing the wonderful felicity of a marriage state, and the admirable pleasures and blessings that ensue thereon: being curious instructions and profitable advice to all young men and maids to lead a peaceful and contented life, when joined in wedlock*	William Seymar
1709	*The Virgin Unmask'd; or, female dialogues betwixt an elderly maiden lady and her niece on love, marriage, memoirs, and morals, etc of the times*	Bernard Mandeville
1714	*Matrimony Unmask'd; or, the comforts and discomforts of marriage display'd*	Edward Ward
1732	*The Genuine Proceedings between the Hon Mrs Weld and her husband in a cause wherein she libels him for impotency, in not consummating the marriage*	Catharine Elizabeth Weld
1740	*The last Speech of Mr Sewell, a degraded Clergyman, who was executed the 29th of November, 1740, for a Clandestine Marriage, etc*	Edward Sewell
1745	*The Pleasures and Felicity of Marriage*	Elizabeth Susanna Davenport Graham
1748	*The Trial wherein Miss D–v–s was Plaintiff, and the Rev Dr W–l–n, Defendant, In an Action of Ten Thousand Pounds for the Non-Performance of a Marriage-Contract; when the Plaintiff had a verdict and recovered Seven Thousand Pounds Damages*	W. Price

---

1   See also page 132 (The Harassing Bridal Tour).

1750	The Fore'd Marriage; or, the miseries and afflicting calamities of the unhappy Miss Betsey Mason	Betsey Mason
1756	Degrees of Marriage; or, an admonition to all such as shall intend hereafter to enter into the state of matrimony, godly and agreeably to the laws set forth	Archbishop of Canterbury
1774	The Legal Degrees of Marriage stated and considered, in a series of letters to a friend	John Alleyne
1774	New reflections on the errors committed in both sexes, before and after Marriage. By a young lady.	F. P.
1778	The Advantages and Disadvantages of the Marriage-State	John Johnson
1780	The Honourableness of Marriage adjusted and defended Together with Observations and Reflections relating to the conduct of married persons	J. Roberts
1780	The lover's new guide; or, a complete library giving full instructions for love, courtship and marriage	Charles Freeman
1784	Reflections on Courtship and Marriage: in two letters to a friend, wherein a practical plan is laid down for observing and securing conjugal felicity	Benjamin Franklin
1792	Useful Hints to Single Gentlemen, Respecting Marriage, Concubinage, and Adultery: in prose and verse	Little Isaac
1801	The Mutual Duties of Husbands and Wives: a sermon occasioned by the marriage of R-------- S------- esq, of M—, preached in Argyle Chapel, Bath, August 16th, 1801	William Jay
1811	Dick Versus Dick; or, a full and curious account of the particular and interesting proceedings, instituted at Doctors' Commons, by Rachael Dick against her husband, the Rev. William Dick, of West Cowes, in the Isle of Wight, for a nullity of marriage, on the ground of impotence; together with the sentence pronounced by Sir John Nichol, on Friday, the twenty-fourth of May, 1811	T. Broom
1812	Advice to Young Persons, Particularly Females, Respecting Marriage: in which the unhappy effects of female vanity and pride, and the good consequences of prudence and virtue, are exemplified in familiar dialogues	R. Shepherd
1813	The Duties, Advantages, Pleasures, and Sorrows of the Marriage State	John Ovington
1815	The Whole Duty of Women; or, a guide to the female sex, from the age of sixteen to sixty, shewing women, of all conditions, how to behave themselves for obtaining not only present but future happiness; by a Lady. To which is added, the Advantages and disadvantages of the marriage state.	William Kenrick
1820	The Illegal Marriage; or, the Adventures of a young lady of fortune who was seduced from her parents by a military officer; and, with her children perished in the forests of America	James Williams
1822	A true and particular account of a shocking, cruel and barbarous attempt to murder Jane Jusland, a servant-girl, by John Bolt who made her offers of marriage, and because she refused, he shot at her with a large traveling pistol, which maimed her in a most shocking manner	W. Stephenson

1824	*A father's advice to his daughter, on entering into the marriage state*	Samuel Thompson
1837	*The Philosophy of Marriage, in its social, moral and physical relations; with an account of the diseases of the genito-urinary organs, and the physiology of generation in the vegetable and animal kingdoms, being part of a course of obstetric lectures delivered at the North London School of Medicine*	Michael Ryan
1838	*The influence of the present marriage system upon the character and interests of females contrasted with that proposed by Robert Morrison*	Mrs Frances Morrison
1842	*The Marriage Question; or, the Lawfulness of marrying the sister of a deceased wife, considered*	Parsons Cook
1842	*The Marriage Ring; or, how to make home happy*	John Angell James
1847	*The Marriage Offering; or, a series of letters addressed to a young married lady, embodying hints on the performance of household duties and on the management of children. By a Widow.*	Anonymous
1848	*The Lawfulness of Marriage with a Deceased Wife's Sister examined by Scripture in a letter to a friend*	Charles Joseph Goodhart
1849	*The Report of Her Majesty's Commission on the Laws of Marriage, relative to marriage with a deceased wife's sister, examined in a letter to Sir R. H. Inglis*	Alexander James Beresford Hope
1849	*The sound policy of the existing Law of Marriage as prohibiting the union of a Widower with his deceased Wife's Sister vindicated*	George Wray
1854	*Marriage: its history, character and results*	Thomas Low Nichols and Mary Gove Nichols
1854	*The Manual of Matrimony and Connubial Companion. By a Bachelor.*	Anonymous
1857	*The sacredness of Christian marriage, and the sin and danger of divorce: a sermon*	William Josiah Irons
1859	*The marriage that will suit you, and how to enjoy it*	Rev. J. W. Howell
1859	*The Etiquette of Love, Courtship and Marriage. To which is added, the etiquette of politeness.*	Anonymous
1863	*The Marriage Gift Book and Bridal Token*	Jabez Burns
1864	*The Young Men and Women's nuptial guide, and physiological view of marriage*	Robert David Lalor
1871	*Matrimony; or, what marriage life is, and how to make the best of it*	John Maynard
1875	*Marriage for the Million for the lads and lasses of the working classes*	Henry Butter
1878	*Cupid's Yokes; or, the binding forces of conjugal life. An essay to consider some moral and physiological phases of love and marriage, wherein is asserted the natural right and necessity of sexual self-government*	Ezra H. Heywood
1883	*The Marriage Ring. A gift-book for the newly-married and for those contemplating marriage*	William Landels

HOW TO BE HAPPY THOUGH MARRIED

IT is the best title for a book in the history of the universe: *How To Be Happy Though Married.* Why no one has made it into a film yet is a mystery. The book was written by the Reverend E. J. Hardy in 1885, and some of its most notable chapters include 'On Making the Best of a Bad Matrimonial Bargain', 'Marriage Considered as a Discipline of Character', 'The Management of Servants' and 'What is the Use of a Child?' There is also a chapter about politeness:

---

1   See below.

True courtesy exhibits itself in a disposition to contribute to the happiness of others, and in refraining from all that may annoy them. And the cultivation day by day of this sweet reasonableness is almost as necessary to the comfort of those who live together as the daily calls of the milkman and the baker. If no two people have it so much in their power to torment each other as husband and wife, it is their bounden duty to guard against this liability by cultivating the habit of domestic politeness. It is a mistake to suppose that the forms of courtesy can be safely dispensed with in the family circle. With the disappearance of the forms the reality will too often disappear. The very effort of appearing bright under adverse circumstances is sure to render cheerfulness easier on another occasion.

Good manners like good words cost little and are worth much. They oil the machinery of social life, but more especially of domestic life. If a cheerful 'good morning' and 'good evening' conciliate strangers they are not lost upon a wife. Hardness and repulsiveness of manner originate in want of respect for the feelings of others . . .

Madam! no gentleman is entitled to such distinguished consideration as your husband. Sir! no lady is entitled to such deferential treatment as your wife.

Politeness does seem to be making a comeback, thank goodness. As Caitlin Moran puts it in *How To Be a Woman* (2011), 'Being polite is possibly the greatest daily contribution everyone can make to life on Earth.' This undoubtedly applies to marriage too. One may feel a bit ridiculous creeping around the house saying 'Excuse me' and 'Would you mind awfully . . . ?', and 'please' and 'thank you' and 'well done', but making such gestures does maintain a certain standard to which surely the human race must aspire. Otherwise, what hope is there?

THE ETIQUETTE OF THE BATHROOM

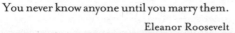

You never know anyone until you marry them.

Eleanor Roosevelt

THE secret to a happy marriage? Separate bathrooms. But if, in these financially challenged times, this proves fiscally impossible, as it does for most of us, then one must find another way to coexist in the realm of personal hygiene.

You might be duped into believing that cohabitation in advance of matrimony, as is the cosmopolitan vogue, equips you with intimate knowledge of the hygiene habits of the modern male. Wrong! Oh, woefully wrong! Scarcely has the last flake of confetti fallen than horrible truth will out. Not a few are the horrified brides who, on what ought to be the most romantic night of their lives, stumble upon their handsome honeymoon beau mid-toilet, or unashamedly sniffing his morning suit stockings as he slips into something more comfortable. It appears that the niceties that prevailed before getting hitched are instantly deemed as pointless and unnecessary as so many discarded wedding favours. Now is the time to steel yourself for a lifetime's exposure to an embarrassment of visceral and gruesome activities of the type more typically associated with a boys' school dormitory.

For your new husband, a fascination with effluvia reigns (from the olfactory to the malleable). Furthermore, many are those who harbour an interest in bodily functions to rival that of most medical laboratory research associates. Your home now is the scene of a veritable conference-worth of probing, investigations, dissections and experimentation. And guess what? You, lady bride, have been unwittingly appointed biological co-researcher. As toenails are held up for inspection, beard shavings line your (previously immaculate) sink for closer perusal, toilets are not ideally flushed (thereby enabling optimal observation of your loved one's digestive events), you may begin to wonder to what you have signed up. Where has that other man gone? The one who smelt delicious, showered every day, locked the bathroom door and ran a tap (so that's why there was never any hot water left!) to disguise his more ebullient lavatorial expressions. Where is he?

You might catch a glimpse of him if you were to spy on him at work, or invite him to your grandmother's, or accompany him to dine with an important client. Or not, if he is some sort of artist or works for a particularly laid-back employer. Perhaps there is no grandmother to force him into shape. It is possible that it was solely for your benefit that he previously strove to maintain a facade of decency and properness. A sorry situation indeed, this. For now you know that he is gone forever, and that that shiny, fragrant, manicured specimen is relegated to some sweet past realm. But know that you are not alone. You have joined the ranks of long-suffering, Dettol-wielding ladies limping through a soup of biological products to carve out something resembling a respectable home. Wondering, in your new involuntary role as lab technician, if men really *are* from Mars, and how likely is it that the flowing liquid found on that planet is water?

One single decision will ease the transition enormously, however. Hire a cleaner. Even if it means not only sacrificing all your liberal principles but also going without food or heat to pay for the privilege. What you spend on a cleaner you will save on the cost of marriage therapy, by avoiding all those boring fights about whose turn it is to clean the loo. There is one final point to note, though: whilst leaving the cap off the toothpaste is forgivable (these days you can buy toothpaste that comes with the cap attached, so it is actually a fight not even really worth having), if either of you fails to hang up your towel for more than two days in a row, you need to get a divorce. At once. Ideally, that very day, if the flight schedule to Reno allows. For there is simply no excuse for this appalling breach of the marriage contract (the unspoken bit, anyway), and it strongly suggests that the perpetrator is, sad to say, a lost cause. If they do not hang up their own towel, imagine the other depravities that lie beneath the surface, just waiting to be revealed as the marriage progresses. Get out now, whilst you still can.

TILL DEATH DO US PART; OR, THREE FAMOUS, HAPPILY MARRIED COUPLES

HAPPY marriages. It is a topic that in real life is discussed depressingly rarely, yet (newsflash) they do exist. It is just that people do not admit to them much — rather sensibly in fact, because who wants to hear talk about the hilarious time you both sent each other flowers on the same day or the fascinating tale of how you happily and equally divide the housework without a cross word between you? No one, that's who. It just sounds like showing off; it probably *is* showing off. It is certainly not funny or interesting (for the same reason, one rarely hears about how great motherhood is; again, it is not funny or interesting). Instead, let us look outside our immediate circle of friends for inspiration, direction and the courage to pursue what sometimes may seem like a rather rarely attained goal. Although one can never be sure which couples are happy together and which are not (it being impossible to know what goes on behind closed doors and all), evidence suggests that the three creative couples below were pretty much the perfect match.

MARIE AND PIERRE CURIE

Marie Skłodowska met Pierre Curie in 1894 while she was studying at the Sorbonne in Paris and he was teaching and researching at the École de Physique et Chimie nearby. They immediately bonded over how much they both adored their work, viewing it as life's main source of happiness. A year later they were married at the town hall in Sceaux, where Pierre's parents lived. Marie wore a simple navy-blue suit that she subsequently wore to work in the laboratory every day for a decade or so — after all, the colour meant that it did not show the stains too much. After the wedding, the Curies went on honeymoon, bicycling their way around Brittany on bicycles they had been given as a wedding present. They quickly returned to the lab, though, where he supported her in the most wonderful way, learning her native language of Polish and giving up his own research to join her in hers. They were soon making hugely important scientific discoveries together, in particular in the field of radioactivity (a word they invented). Marie later wrote that she and Pierre were entirely absorbed in the new field that opened up before us, thanks to the discovery so little expected. And we were very happy in spite of the difficult conditions under which we worked. We passed our days at the laboratory, often eating a simple student's lunch there. A great tranquillity reigned in our poor shabby hangar; occasionally, while observing an operation, we would walk up and down talking of our work, present and future. When we were cold, a cup of hot tea, drunk beside the stove, cheered us. We lived in a preoccupation as complete as that of a dream.

In 1903, the Curies were jointly awarded the Nobel Prize for Physics. But tragically, just three years later, Pierre was knocked down and killed by a horse-drawn wagon as he crossed the rue Dauphine near the Pont Neuf in heavy rain. On that day, Marie wrote, 'I lost my beloved Pierre, and with him all hope and all support for the rest of my life.' She was left alone to raise their two daughters, Irène aged nine and Ève aged two, but she still managed to win the Nobel Prize for Chemistry in 1911, thereby becoming the only person ever to win a Nobel Prize in two different sciences. She died in 1934 at the age of sixty-six of the effects of radiation.

JAMES AND NORA JOYCE

They met in the street, on Nassau Street in Dublin to be precise, on 10 June 1904, when he was twenty-two and she was twenty and still named Nora Barnacle. Despite (or because of?) the fact he was not wearing his glasses, it was love at first sight, according to them both. She agreed to meet him the following Tuesday at 8.30 p.m. outside Sir William Wilde's house on Merrion Square, but did not turn up, so their first date took place instead on 16 June — the day on which *Ulysses* is set, later commemorated as Bloomsday. Below is a note she wrote him during the early days of their courtship while she was working as a chambermaid at Finn's Hotel in Dublin.

> Dear Jim
>
> I feel so very tired to night I can't say much many thanks for your kind letter which I received unexpectedly this evening I was very busy when the Post-man came I ran off to one of the bedroom's to read your letter I was called five times but did not pretend to hear it is now half past eleven and I need not tell you I can hardly keep my eyes open and I am delighted to sleep the night away when I cant be thinking of you so much when I awake in the morning I will think of nothing but you Good night till 7pm to morrow eve
>
> Nora xxxxxxxxx

Nora's writing style leaves no doubt that Joyce later based the stream-of-consciousness style of Molly Bloom in *Ulysses* on her, and anyone who claims otherwise is either silly or sexist or both. Within just a few months of meeting, the couple ran away to Zurich together, but the job he had set up there fell through and they immediately had to up sticks to Trieste, where he found another position teaching English. From then on, they were almost always together and hence little correspondence between them exists, although in 1909 they wrote a flurry of brilliantly filthy letters to each other that opened with lines like his 'My sweet little naughty fuckbird'. They argued, of course, sometimes furiously, and the marriage had its tensions, strains, and unresolved and irresolvable issues, just as all long-term partnerships do. In essence, though, theirs was an exceptionally happy marriage, and friends later testified how much they loved and depended upon each other and enjoyed being together. He died in 1941 and she died ten years later, leaving behind a daughter Lucia, a son Georgio and a grandson Stephen.

LIONEL BULMER AND MARGARET GREEN

Their friends called them 'Margaretandlionel' because they did everything together, which is either utterly sweet or utterly claustrophobic and diminishing, depending on your point of view. He was born in 1919 in London, the son of an architect; she was born in 1925 in West Hartlepool, the daughter of a worker in a steel plant who ran an art club on the side. They both won scholarships to the Royal College of Art, which had been evacuated to the Lake District because of the Second World War, and it was there that they fell in love. (Who doesn't fall in love when they're in the Lake District? On a sunny day, there is nowhere more beautiful on the planet. And see page 133 [on honeymoons].) They were married, and spent their life painting together, first in Chelsea and later in Suffolk. they were among the most interesting figurative painters of their generation. The writer Ann Baer, who was a friend of theirs, remarked, 'In no other couple did I ever hear so little "I" and so much "we".' Following Lionel's death in 1992, Margaret was so heartbroken that she did not complete another painting for the entire remaining eleven years of her life. In recent years the two of them have been championed by Messum's, an art gallery on Cork Street in Mayfair; works of theirs are sometimes available there for under £1,000, which may prove useful information if one of your richer relatives or friends asks you for ideas for a wedding present.

THE MARITAL BED

THERE are those who insist that the key to wedded bliss is to sleep in the biggest bed possible. They are wrong. It is, conversely, to sleep in the smallest bed possible: that way, whatever comings and goings daylight brings, when night falls you are *forced* into some sort of physical closeness. This is far healthier, emotionally, than the alternative, which is occasionally to holler across an acre of sheets, 'Hello? You there? Fancy a rumble?' When it comes to the brand of bed, Savoir or Vi-Spring are the luxury choice, and if you are having a wedding gift list be sure to include the most expensive new duvet and pillows you can bear to ask for without feeling ashamed. But for the best advice, let us turn to that hallowed British institution John Lewis, whose existence alone is reason enough never to move abroad. After all, nothing really bad could ever happen to you in a John Lewis. Definitely the first port of call if there is ever a nuclear attack.

HOW TO BUY A BED, ACCORDING TO JOHN LEWIS

Try! We always recommend that you try out a bed before ordering online or by phone.

Comfortably numb? A good way to check if the bed you are lying on is too soft, too hard, or just right is to lie on your back, placing your hand in the small of your back and then trying to move it about. If it moves too easily, the bed may be too hard for you; if it's a struggle to move your hand, then the bed is too soft. If you can move your hand with just a little resistance, the bed may be just right for you.

Take it easy Take some time out and lie down. You spend a third of your life in bed, so it's vital that you make the right choice.

Roll with it Try the bed in all of the sleeping positions you tend to use, not only on your back, and try a selection of beds for comparison.

It takes two If you share a bed, take your partner with you. Remember, it's important a new bed suits both of you.

Different types of bed
- *Divans* act as bases for mattresses and either have springs which allow the mattress to adapt to the body's contours, or a solid top which provides firmer support. A divan is useful if you're tight on space as most are available with drawers to provide additional storage.
- *Bedsteads* are more decorative and will provide a definite classic or contemporary look to your bedroom. A 'bowed slat' (or 'sprung slat') bedstead will give more cushioned support than a 'solid slat'.

- *A headboard* is of course an optional extra — most of our divans are sold without so you have a more flexible choice.
- *Storage beds* feature built-in drawers that free up valuable space in other parts of the bedroom. Another space-saving feature is Ottoman storage — revealed by opening the top of the bed with an easy-to-operate mechanism.

Points to consider

- *A bed is an important investment* . . . especially when you consider that every £100 you spend on a bed represents just 2.7p a night over 10 years.
- *The best bed for you isn't necessarily the most expensive bed* . . . though it's worth spending as much as you can afford to get a really good mattress.
- *The average lifespan of a bed* . . . or at least the mattress, is about 8–10 years. After regular use a bed may have deteriorated by as much as 75% from its original condition.
- *An old bed isn't hygienic* . . . we sweat as much as half to a full pint of fluid a night, and house dust mites accumulate in beds too.
- *Consider the space you need at night.* While you may plump for a standard double bed, a W150 x L200cm kingsize bed gives couples more room to relax and stretch out during sleep.

Measuring up

John Lewis beds are available in all UK standard sizes. The dimensions of a bedstead are greater than a divan base equivalent, but the mattress size required remains the same. The mattresses we sell are sized as shown.

Mattress name	Mattress size
Small single	W75 x L190cm
Single	W90 x L190cm
Small double	W120 x L190cm
Double	W135 x L190cm
Kingsize	W150 x L200cm
Super kingsize	W180 x L200cm
Super kingsize zipped and linked	W180 x L200cm

There are other advantages to shopping for a bed in a department store. In *The Winds of Heaven* by Monica Dickens (1955), lonely widow Louisa meets a kind, older man in a Lyons teashop, and later tracks him down to an Oxford Street department store, where he works as a bed salesman.

One afternoon, walking among the vacant, pushing crowds in Oxford Street, Louise was so bored with herself that she turned into the shop where Gordon Disher worked, and took the lift to the bed department. She wandered among the rows of beds that offered themselves bleakly to the human body, but there was no sign of the breathless, fat man with the gentle voice. An assistant came up, and Louise asked nervously for Mr Disher, trying to sound like a customer . . .

He came towards her, moving among the supine beds assuredly, like an elephant shouldering its way through a familiar jungle. When he saw who it was, he increased his pace, and arrived a little out of breath before Louise, in his neglected dark suit that surely only just scraped by the standards of the store. Did one shake hands? He solved the problem for her by holding out his hand. 'I'm delighted to see you,' he said, in that soft voice, which could not help sounding intimate. 'I didn't think I would.' . . .

The department was as empty as furniture departments invariably are, so that, walking through them, you wonder how the store can afford to keep so much stock. There were only the beds, without character now, but each waiting to become the centre of someone's existence; the haven for tired limbs and plagued minds, the resting-place for sickness, the battle-ground for love.

'I'm sure I shouldn't keep you talking,' Louise said, seeing the glance. 'Unless, of course, I buy a bed, and I don't really need one . . .'

I shall ask him to tea, she thought. Next Sunday, when Eva is out. She won't mind. She said she was going to Richmond. I shall ask him to tea and buy a lemon cake and make sandwiches. When she asked him, he accepted at once . . . He seemed delighted. He leaned his fat hand on a nearby bed and prodded the springs, smiling like a boy offered a treat.

An assistant was approaching with a sheaf of papers. 'Till Sunday, then.' Louise held out her hand, and was going to take it back, recollecting that this would not do before another assistant, but Gordon Disher took it and held it softly for a second, his own hand quite enveloping it. Evidently, he had been here long enough to have favourite customers, who came to him through the years for marriage beds, cots, beds for daughters getting married, cots for grandchildren, until they were on handshaking terms with our Mr Disher.

Not that, at this stage in your life, you are likely to be on the lookout for a new man. One hopes.

RELIGIOUS WRITER WLTM . . . ; OR, THE PERFECT WIFE, ACCORDING TO THE BIBLE

Who can find a virtuous woman? For her price is far above rubies. The heart of her husband doth safely trust in her, so that he shall have no need of spoil. She will do him good and not evil all the days of her life. She seeketh wool, and flax, and worketh willingly with her hands. She is like the merchants' ships; she bringeth her food from afar. She riseth also while it is yet night, and giveth meat to her household, and a portion to her maidens. She considereth a field, and buyeth it: with the fruit of her hands she planteth a vineyard. She girdeth her loins with strength, and strengtheneth her arms. She perceiveth that her merchandise is good: her candle goeth not out by night. She layeth her hands to the spindle, and her hands hold the distaff. She stretcheth out her hand to the poor; yea, she reacheth forth her hands to the needy. She is not afraid of the snow for her household: for all her household are clothed with scarlet. She maketh herself coverings of tapestry; her clothing is silk and purple. Her husband is known in the gates, when he sitteth among the elders of the land. She maketh fine linen, and selleth it; and delivereth girdles unto the merchant. Strength and honour are her clothing; and she shall rejoice in time to come. She openeth her mouth with wisdom; and in her tongue is the law of kindness. She looketh well to the ways of her household, and eateth not the bread of idleness. Her children arise up, and call her blessed; her husband also, and he praiseth her.

Proverbs 31:10–27

DISHWASHER WARS

NOW to that most thorny of marital topics, especially amongst newly-weds. No, not that of in-laws or Christmas traditions, or who was friends with Pete first. Forget disagreements over paint colour, money spent on haircuts or turning work shirts pink by mistake. It is true, though, that the battle in question is indeed also fought on that most thorny of plains: where dirty goes in and clean emerges. Yet no mere washing machine or attendant 'issues' rival the levels of aggression and hostility brought about by that king of household appliances (Lo! There *is* something that leaves one's hands softer than Fairy!): the dishwasher. For many of us, it is the first joint purchase we make together as a couple, and we both kneel before its hallowed altar. But each of us also defends our unique and idiosyncratic style of said worshipping to the death. Here, then, follows the simple, official guide, as recommended by *manufacturers themselves*, to loading one's filthy and beloved crockery to achieve maximum sparkle.

1. *'No, that stuff goes on the top!'*
Experts advise: The top rack is for less soiled items, along with cups and glasses. NB This has been tested and (infuriatingly) found to be true. The bottom rack is for the dirtiest stuff. (Argh, al*right*!)

2. *'Go on, just squeeze it in. It's not going to smash . . .'*
Experts advise: In order to ensure that one's tableware is protected from chips and scratches, overpacking should definitely be avoided. (Tch — it's only *water* in there . . .)

3. *Ah. This one. This can get nasty. To position utensils facing up or down?*
Experts advise: Apart from sharp knives (which should generally be concealed in safes at loading hours, in any case), utensils
should be placed with dirty bit face up. (Ha! *Told you!*) Knives
should apparently adopt a horizontal pose in the top rack (thus
some posh models have dedicated cutlery trays these days).

4. *'Oh, they'll go in there. That's fine. I always put those long-handled spoons
in the confusingly miscellaneous cutlery bit.'*
Experts advise: Long-handled spoons etc. should be kept well
out of the way of the 'spray arms'. (Whatever the heck *they* are
– well, why don't you just *look in the manual*? Or not. You never
will. You never do. That's *the problem*. Or rather, one of the
many . . .)

5. *'The instructions? What? Oh, I recycled them . . .'*
Experts advise: The 'manufacturer's instructions' should be
pored over before placing one's crockery and utensils in the
Machine of Wonder, to maximize water circulation and
thereby ensure that every item enjoys optimal exposure to its
cleansing properties.

MARRIAGE PROBLEMS,
VIA THE CLASSIFIEDS

ALL couples fight, but at least be dignified enough to keep your differences private — unlike the men and women below, all of whom apparently decided to inform the entire community of their relationship stumbles via a personal ad in a newspaper. So vulgar!

Whereas my wife, Mary Sermon, being lewdly inclined. And not content with the endearments nature hath afforded me, hath taken into her employ another man; this is to caution all persons not to trust her, as I will not pay any debts she may contract. The Mark of W. Sermon. Witness Benjamin Kiddell.

The Times, 1785

Whereas my wife CHARITY has, without cause, eloped from my bed and board, and persists in a resolution not to live with me: These are to warn all persons not to deal with, or trust her any thing on my account, as I shall not be liable to pay any debts of her contracting after this date; and whereas she may be influenced to such disorderly practices, by the counsel and encouragement of ill-disposed people, all persons are hereby forewarned against harbouring or countenancing her in any respect, that she may be convinced of the indecency and impropriety of her behaviour, and return to her duty. Any person offending against this notification may expect to be dealt with as the law directs. Adam Barr.

Pennsylvania Gazette, 13 July 1785

[Then, a few days later:]

Whereas the subscriber, Wife of Adam Barr, much to her grief, has found her name published in the papers by her husband, accusing her of eloping from him without any cause. If being often beat and abused in a most cruel manner, thrown in the fire, sometimes almost strangled by him, at other times thrown on the floor and stamped on, swearing he would murder her, and other ill treatment, which disabled her from getting out of bed for several days, suffering both black and white servants to abuse her with ill language, and when her mother came to see her, he in a furious manner turned both her and her mother out of doors. If such cruel usage, from a man who ought to have been her best friend, be not sufficient cause for leaving him, she leaves the impartial to judge. Charity Barr.

Pennsylvania Gazette, 10 August 1785

Whereas, Elisabeth Wicks, Wife of Thomas Wicks, left the Parish of Broadwater, upwards of six Months, to go to London, and her Husband is fearful some Misfortune has happened to her. He is likewise apprehensive, that she has either pawned her Clothes, or sold them, and what she had with her, and afraid of coming Home, but my Dear, fear nothing, for if you have not a Shift to your Back, let me know where I may hear of you, and immediately I will bring you Clothes and Money, and will receive you as kind as the Day I was married to you, and will pledge myself never to upbraid you. Thomas Wicks.

The Times, 1790

Whereas my wife Betsey, has eloped from my bed and board and has behavind in an unbecoming and indecent manner, by propagating the human species in a way other than the one

167

prescribed by law; this is to caution all KINDS of people both BLACK, WHITE, or PYE-BALLED, against trusting her on my account, (harbour her they may if they can) as I will not pay one MILLE of her contracting after this date.

Bridgewater, July 30.

John Bolton.

Columbian Sentinel, 1797

Thomas Hutchins has advertised, that I have absented my self from his bed and board, and forbid all persons trusting me on his account, and cautioned all persons against making me any payment on his account. I now advertise the public, that the same Thomas Hutchins came as a fortune-teller into this town about a year ago, with a recommendation, which, with some artful falsehoods, induced me to marry him. Of the four wives he had before me, the last he quarrelled away; how the other three came by their deaths, he can best inform the public; but I caution all widows or maidens against marrying him, be their desire for matrimony ever so strong. Should he make his advances under a feigned name, they may look out for a little, strutting, talkative, feeble, meagre, hatchet-faced fellow, with spindle shanks, and a little warped in the back. East Windsor, May 22, 1807. Thankful Hutchins.

Connecticut Courant, 1807

Run away last night, my wife, Bridget Coole, She is a tight neat body, and has lost one leg. She was seen riding behind the priest of the parish through Fermoy; and, as we never was married, I will pay no debt that she does not contract. She lisps with one tooth, and is always talking about fairies, and is of no use but to the owner. — Phelim Coole, his X mark.

The Times, 1832

Mrs ------n. Your note has been received. It is evasive, cold, and cruel. It is incredible that you should be watched and coerced; if so, come at once to the man who is now fully prepared to be satisfactorily yours only, and for life. What accursed spirit holds you in thraldom, and can influence you to abandon your child and husband? In wretchedness he appeals to you against this influence. Let the feelings of your own good heart prevail. RETURN, if but for a few days, to your home, and confer with your husband. Nothing shall be done to mar your comfort or ease, but do not, for the will of others, sacrifice the peace of mind and health of the man you have professed to love above all others. Your husband, A.F.

The Times, 1851

HOW TO COOK A SUNDAY ROAST

THERE is no more wifely duty than cooking a Sunday roast. For those of us who don't generally cook, roast chicken is one of the few dishes that is not rocket science to cook but looks it. Roasting a chicken is also the gateway to other, even more impressive offerings such as roast beef, lamb, pork, duck, ostrich, flamingo . . .

Place the chicken on a roasting tray and smear it all over with butter, garlic, lemon (the juice, squeezed, and the rind, grated) and thyme. The more the merrier, especially with the butter, since the rule is that the more butter you use, the more delicious the chicken will be. Cook it in an oven preheated to 200°C for about forty-five minutes for each kilogram of chicken, plus an extra twenty minutes for luck. Don't forget to baste it occasionally.

Then spruce the meal up with some chic and unexpected vegetables from a farmers' market. Reject staid, boring broccoli or carrots in favour of green beans mixed with vibrant red beetroot stalks or cauliflower fried in chilli and garlic. A green salad is also strangely delicious with a roast, and rather elegant in its boldness. To avoid the horror of sitting down to said lunch utterly exhausted and bad-tempered, consider peeling (or 'prepping', in chef's terms) all the vegetables the day before. The potatoes will then need to be kept in a bowl of water overnight, but all the others will be just fine in the fridge in plastic bags or Tupperware boxes. Remember that roast potatoes always take longer to cook than you think, so start them early. When the moment strikes, boil the potatoes for 5–10 minutes and then drain them in a colander, shaking the colander vigorously in order to roughen up the outsides. Nigella has an excellent tip here, which is to sprinkle the potatoes with semolina to make them extra crispy. Then add them to the roasting tray with the chicken and cook for about an hour, turning once, until crispy.

The tricky bit is the timing — that is, making sure everything's ready at approximately the same time. But the roast chicken can happily sit beneath aluminium foil for fifteen minutes or more, so that gives one a bit of breathing space, and then there are just the vegetables to wrestle with. This is the moment to take people up on their offer of help: decanting into dishes, adding a knob of butter or a slosh of olive oil, searching for serving spoons. All the while, you need to make the gravy in whatever way your mother or a TV chef has passed down to you; one tip is to use a whisk to ensure the gravy is super-smooth, and also to add cream or crème fraîche for extra richness. By the time it is all on the table, you will feel as triumphant as if you have just performed brain surgery. Finally, try offering your guests lime pickle from the local Indian shop to accompany the chicken: it will be a culinary revelation for all those present, guaranteed. Entire cooking empires have been built on less.

YOU JUST DON'T UNDERSTAND

DEBORAH Tannen's seminal book *You Just Don't Understand: Women and Men in Conversation* ought to be compulsory reading for all couples. First published in 1990, it is the book that hundreds of abysmal yet mystifyingly best-selling so-called 'self-help' manuals about 'relationships' (even the word 'relationships' is a naff one) have since ripped off for its insights into the differing ways men and women communicate. For example, Tannen, a professor at Georgetown University in Washington, DC, was the first to point out that most men do not like to ask for directions, now a standard of comedy routines the world over. Here are three of the book's most eye-opening passages:

I'LL FIX IT FOR YOU

Women and men are both often frustrated by the other's way of responding to their expression of troubles. And they are further hurt by the other's frustrations. If women resent men's tendency to offer solutions to problems, men complain about women's refusal to take action to solve the problems they complain about. Since many men see themselves as problem solvers, a complaint or a trouble is a challenge to their ability to think of a solution, just as a woman presenting a broken bicycle or stalling car poses a challenge to their ingenuity in fixing it. But whereas many women appreciate help in fixing mechanical equipment, few are inclined to appreciate help 'fixing' emotional problems . . . Trying to solve a problem or fix a trouble focuses on the message level of talk. But for most women who habitually report problems at work or in friendships, the message is not the main point of complaining. It's the metamessage that counts. Telling about a problem is a bid for an expression of understanding ('I know how you feel') or a similar complaint ('I felt the same way when something similar happened to me'). In other words, troubles talk is intended to reinforce rapport by sending the metamessage 'We're the same; you're not alone.' Women are frustrated when they not only don't get this reinforcement but, quite the opposite, feel distanced by the advice, which seems to send the metamessage 'We're not the same. You have the problems; I have the solutions.'

DON'T ASK

Why do many men resist asking for directions and other kinds of information? And, it is just as reasonable to ask, why is it that many women don't? . . . If relations are inherently hierarchical, then the one who has more information is framed as higher up on the ladder, by virtue of being more knowledgeable and competent. From this perspective, finding one's own way is an essential part of the independence that men perceive to be a prerequisite for self-respect. If self-respect is bought at the cost of a few extra minutes of travel time, it is well worth the price . . . Insofar as giving information frames one as the expert, superior in knowledge, and the other as uninformed, inferior in knowledge, it is a move in the negotiation of status.

PUT DOWN THAT PAPER AND TALK TO ME!

For most women, the language of conversation is primarily a language of rapport: a way of establishing connections and negotiating relationships. Emphasis is placed on displaying similarities and matching experiences . . . For most men, talk is primarily a means to preserve independence and negotiate and maintain status in a hierarchical social order. This is done by exhibiting knowledge and skill, and by holding centre stage through verbal performance such as storytelling, joking or imparting information . . .

For everyone, home is a place to be offstage. But the comfort of home can have opposite and incompatible meanings for women and men. For many men, the comfort of home means freedom from having to prove themselves and impress through verbal display. At last, they are in a situation where talk is not required. They are free to remain silent. But for women, home is a place where they are free to talk, and where they feel greatest need for talk, with those they are closest to. For them, the comfort of home means the freedom to talk without worrying about how their talk will be judged . . .

Understanding the differing views can help detoxify the situation, and both can make adjustments. Realising that men and women have different assumptions about the place of talk in relationships, a woman can observe a man's desire to read the morning paper at the breakfast table without interpreting it as a rejection of her or a failure of their relationship. And a man can understand a woman's desire for talk without interpreting it as an unreasonable demand or a manipulative attempt to prevent him from doing what he wants to do.

Tannen's basic message is that most fights are caused by miscommunication. People normally aren't being horrible or wrong; they just communicate differently. It's nobody's fault necessarily, rather it's the way we are wired. Buy her book today: it'll save you thousands in divorce lawyers tomorrow.

AMIES SANS MARIS (ASM); OR, YOUR FRIENDS WITHOUT HUSBANDS

NOW that you are officially shackled to your Old Pot and Pan (your man, for those not *au fait* with cockney rhyming slang), maintaining your relationships with your friends who are not married can be a minefield. In your world it has become horrifyingly normal to debate the likes of 'What's the earliest time one is allowed to retire to bed without it being embarrassing?', yet in your friend's world, this is just more evidence that you have once and for all gone over to the dark side: wifedom. Here, then, are some tips on how to avoid losing your dear *amies sans maris* (ASM) forever.

THE TEN RULES OF ENGAGEMENT

I. *Thou shalt not be smug.* No one wants to see that altogether transparent tendency so associated with newly-weds emanating from their once-normal friend. And smugness is at its worst when attempts are made to disguise it. Whenever you feel the need to yap about your blissful situation, even if you were planning to hide it behind another statement, don't. Sadly, it won't take much for your single friends to sort of hate you right now. A patronizing 'Oh dear – again?' when one of them tells you she has just been dumped comes with its own little neon arrow pointing to the traces of a smile that *you just can't keep inside.* And no amount of sympathetic stroking and patting will distract her from it.

2. *Thou shalt not discuss thy husband unless asked directly,* which is rare. Once hitched, nobody ever asks, 'So, how's it going?' in the way they do with regard to a boyfriend. Rather, there seems to be an assumption that it is somehow impolite to imply anything other than constant marital bliss, as though the moment you get married all relationship problems just magically disappear – which, of course, they most certainly do not. Or perhaps, understandably, the subject just becomes too boring to anyone other than the two protagonists. Which is an entirely fair position to adopt, in the circumstances.

3. *Thou shalt not make value judgements about how having a husband is harder than being single.* Because it *isn't*, remember? Cast your mind back to the last time you had 'flu before meeting him. Wasn't it awful? No one cared *that much*. Your 'best friend' would say things like, 'Where *were* you last week, anyway?' To which you would incredulously – though still weakly – retort, 'In bed, with a temperature of 50 degrees,' and she'd say, 'Oh, yeah . . .' It's really hard to be single. The fun or funny thing that just happened becomes far juicier upon sharing it with someone who is legally obliged to laugh.

4. *Thou shalt not bemoan a lack of social life.* Either get out again and stop mooning about in the house together, or else accept that there now exists a ready-made social life, which is free and cosy and just sitting there, behind one's front door.

5. *Thou shalt not criticize other couples.* Particularly in front of single friends. Bizarrely, married people seem to do this before the commencement of procreation. Then they move on to denigrating others' parenting skills, or actual children. The pre-kids bitching includes subjects such as how others choose

to spend money, the amount of 'date nights' they schedule a week (oh please – who coined this appalling term?), where they go on holiday and how often they have sex. It's competitive, presumably, and quite uniquely focused on that time before children pop out. Some sort of tribal, primitive drive? Whatever, it's awful. And weird. Don't do it.

6. *Thou shalt not discuss thy husband with senior colleagues at work, even and especially if they are also considered friends.* Especially single ones. If you have any eye on the higher rungs of the career ladder, just leave him out of it. In any office, a sensitized 'Another One Down!' alarm begins to shriek as soon as a young lady announces her engagement. Do not give bosses any cause to believe that you are dreaming about your domestic situation whilst at work; their minds will travel straight to the day you shyly knock on their door to announce a delightful pregnancy. Just button up and buckle down.

7. *Thou shalt not cite thy husband as a motive for leaving a social occasion early* (at least, not more than once or twice). *Yes*, he will have needs that must (occasionally) be answered. He will place demands on you that your single pals will be unable to comprehend. There will be work dos, and weddings of *his* pals that you really cannot escape now you are formally connected. There will be arduous trips to in-laws, and Saturdays spent decorating, or perhaps a-bed. Your stalwart female crew will accept that, boringly, you do now have another person to consider before rashly booking an all-female holiday to Ibiza, or committing yourself to a day at the spa without first consulting the joint calendar. Or bank account. But do not expect their patience to extend too much beyond the clearly rational. Excuses for rushing off based on 'cooking his supper'

or that he 'likes me to be at home' will not wash. And nor should they. This is the twenty-first century, girlfriend, and the rules have (praise be!) been radically redrafted.

8. *Thou shalt not eschew nights out with the ladies.* These brilliant blow-outs act as balm to any functioning marriage. It goes without saying that your husband then has *carte blanche* to go off and get riotously drunk, or spend a day (though not too many) at comic conventions. Or whatever.

9. *Thou shalt not forget the importance of thy female friendships.* It is these strong and precious female bonds that stand to get you through the rough years and the marital arguments (which will mostly revolve around dishwashers). Only a fool would fail to invest in them at this rose-tinted point.

10. And a note for the ASM herself: *thou too shalt not be too demanding.* For this girl *is* now married. She *does* have to consider the feelings and diary of another human before decision-making. And her friends will need to bear this in mind, before they get too huffy about one of the more reasonable grounds (such as a funeral) for not being able to drop everything to go to a gig or shoe shopping, or have you to stay in the spare room for weeks at a time.

There will no doubt have to be some realignment of previously held habits and comportment. But hopefully not too much, since we trust that you will have selected a sensible chap with his own interests, rather than an irrational psychopath. It helps if your friends and husband get on, since any negotiations can then be achieved in a civilized fashion, rather than in the traumatic style more usually associated with desperate daytime television fiascos.

MOST PUBLISHED PASSAGE ABOUT LOVE AND MARRIAGE EVER (PART 2)[1]

You were born together, and together you shall be forevermore.
You shall be together when the white wings of death scatter your days.
Ay, you shall be together even in the silent memory of God.
But let there be spaces in your togetherness,
And let the winds of heavens dance between you.

Love one another, but make not a bond of love:
Let it rather be a moving sea between the shores of your souls.
Fill each other's cup but drink not from one cup.
Give one another of your bread but eat not from the same loaf.
Sing and dance together and be joyous, but let each one of you be alone,
Even as the strings of a lute are alone though they quiver with the same
    music.

Give your hearts, but not into each other's keeping.
For only the hand of Life can contain your hearts.
And stand together yet not too near together:
For the pillars of the temple stand apart,
And the oak tree and the cypress grow not in each other's shadow.

Khalil Gibran, *The Prophet* (1923)

In essence, don't rely on your husband to make you happy.
Only you yourself can make you happy; he's just the icing on
the penis-shaped cake.

---

1   See also page 24, Most Published Passage about Love and Marriage Ever (Part 1).

HOW TO CHANGE . . .

. . . **NO**, not your husband: if you wanted him to be different you should have married somebody else, frankly. Rather, this is about how to change a plug or other household essentials. The (a?) trouble with marriage is that it makes many of us increasingly incapable as the years recede before us: now that you rarely *have* to carry out such chores in the way you did when you were single, on the rare occasions when you do you find you have completely forgotten how. Pathetic. So here is a quick reminder.

. . . A PLUG

- Dig out a screwdriver from the bottom of the random drawer in which it likes to hide with its friend the international plug adaptor and the old phone charger. Use it to unscrew the centre screw that sits in between the three prongs of the plug.
- Turn the plug over, and take out the now-loosened three screws on the other side that keep the cables in place. Extract these cables, and then throw the old plug away.
- Unscrew the centre screw of the new plug. If you then come across a cord grip, remove this too, and the fuse cartridge if you like because this will make it less fiddly to wire. At this point, double-check the new plug's fuse rating against the appliance it is about to be fitted on, because if these differ it might explode in your face, or similar.

- Now unscrew the screws on the three terminal connections in order to loosen them a little bit. Check for any damage on the sleeving of the cables. The brown one is the 'live' cable and there will be an 'L' marked on the inside of the plug next to the terminal where it is supposed to go. The blue one is the 'neutral' cable and there will be an 'N' marked on the inside of the plug next to the terminal where it is supposed to go. The green and yellow stripy one is the 'earth' cable and there will be an 'E' marked on the inside of the plug next to the terminal where it is supposed to go.
- The easiest way to rewire the cables is in the following order: neutral, earth, live. Insert the end of each cable into its correct terminal, ensuring that you push each all the way and that there is no bare wire showing outside the terminal. Each wire should lie flat and not be squished or damaged.
- Replace the fuse cartridge and insert the main cable into the gripping that's found at the plug's opening. Screw the terminal screws back in, replace the plug's cover and tighten the centre screw.
- *Et, voilà.* Now all that's left to be done is to bask in one's own brilliance with a G&T in one hand and the screwdriver in the other. A harbinger of a night of fun for any red-blooded male who happens to walk in the door at that particular moment, surely.

. . . A TYRE

- First, do your best to break down somewhere convenient like in a pub car park, rather than, say, on the side of a country lane in Cornwall. Second, try to be efficient enough actually to have a spare tyre with you – and no, not round your husband's waist, ha ha.

- Make sure the car is in reverse gear and apply the hand-brake, and ensure that you are parked off the road and in the safest spot possible – and one that is ideally level, firm and not wet or muddy. Turn the hazard lights on. Take the keys out and keep them on you. Ask all passengers to get out of the car and stand on the side of the road, calling out annoyingly unhelpful advice. Ideally, place a log or plank of wood or something on either side of the tyre opposite the one you're changing and also the one diagonally opposite. This is to make sure the car does not roll away at an inconvenient moment.

- Locate the spare tyre and all the tools you need. Usually you'll find them if you lift up the base of the boot.

- Use the tyre iron[1] to loosen the nuts that hold the wheel to the hub of the car. Place the tyre iron on one of the nuts and then put your foot on it and use the pressure of your whole body weight to loosen the nut, maybe even pumping it up and down at first to persuade the iron to shift. To loosen the nut you want to be unscrewing to the left – that is, anti-clockwise.

---

1   To spare any embarrassment, a tyre iron looks like this:

Tyres tend to be on tightly, very very tightly, and even rusted on if it's an old car, in which case you are unlikely to be able to do it yourself – 'I simply couldn't do it, the nuts were rusted on' is a good excuse in almost any context, you'll find. Loosen, but do not unscrew entirely.

- Right, deep breath: now the jacking part. This is what puts many people off having a go themselves in the first place, but in the depths of Cornwall you may have no choice. Position the jack under the car, pushed up against the car's frame; if the car has a dedicated slot – a 'jacking point' – next to the tyre which the top of the jack fits into, as many do these days, make sure the top of the jack is directly underneath it. Then get to work. Twist the jack's lever clockwise, or if there isn't one then attach the tyre iron to the jack and use that to turn the jack until it begins to rise and raise the car off the ground. Don't be alarmed by the deafening creaking noises like the stairs of a pantomime haunted house: that's normal. Keep going until the car is so high that the tyre you need to change is fully raised off the ground. A second jack can come in very useful at this point if the tyre proves difficult to remove from the axle.

- Next, use your hands to unscrew the loosened nuts on the tyre the rest of the way (be sure to put them somewhere safe immediately where you won't lose them) and then remove the flat tyre. Wipe off any dirt or mud on the hub with a cloth or an old tissue.

- Lift up the new tyre, match up the holes on its rim to the bolts on the car, and then hold it in place while you use your hands to tighten the nuts as much as you can. This bit can be tricky and involve a bit of balancing on your knees, etc.

- Now lower the jack by turning the lever anti-clockwise until the car is back resting on the ground as normal. Remove the jack, and then use the tyre iron to tighten the nuts even more.

After whichever one you do first, next do the one diagonally across from it; and repeat, to make sure that the tyre is tightened evenly and does not wobble when the vehicle is driven.

- Put the flat tyre back where you found the spare and make sure the tools are safe and secure so that they don't fly out and give anyone concussion. Then flee to a garage as soon as you can to obtain a permanent replacement. Drive extra carefully, though, and no faster than 50 miles per hour.

... A LIGHT BULB

Really? Surely no need to detail this one, however unmanly and unhandy him indoors may be, so instead I leave you with a joke:

Q. How many newly-weds does it take to change a light bulb?

A. None: they prefer it dark.

A. Two: one to change the light bulb, the other to praise the changing of the bulb.

A. Forever and infinity: 'I'll change the bulb for you', 'No, I'll change the bulb for you', 'No, *I*'ll change the bulb for you' . . .

SEVEN RANDOM MUSINGS
ON HOW TO STAY HAPPILY MARRIED

1. *Marry the right person.* Granted, this is not terribly helpful advice; it is, however, the best advice out there, and thus worth repeating. Not only does the man you marry need to be the right person; he also needs to want the same things as you. Love, unfortunately, is not enough. You must also have broadly similar visions of where you want to live, whether or not you want children, how you envisage spending your retirement and so on. These issues can make or break a marriage, however much romance was involved at the beginning. Oh, and if you are lucky enough to marry the right person, keep quiet about it. A happy marriage is a delicate, precious entity, and if set loose into the universe too often, who knows when it might shatter. Nurture it, appreciate it, but whatever you do, try not to talk about it out loud too often. To do so is to tempt fate.

2. *Learn to argue properly.* According to almost all studies of relationships, this is by far the most important element of a successful marriage. The great Tolstoy concurred: 'What counts in making a happy marriage is not so much how compatible you are, but how you deal with incompatibility.' There are endless cheesy 'self-help' books on this subject, but the most important advice offered in most of them is pretty specific: try to minimize the accusatory use of the pronoun 'you' in favour of 'I' or 'me'. So, '*I* feel angry and ignored when . . .' or 'It upsets *me* when . . .', rather than '*You* do this' or '*You* are always that . . .' This approach really makes a difference to the

direction a heated discussion takes. In addition, and just as (if not more) crucial, avoid a tone of contempt – which, according to research by the Gottman Institute, is the no. 1 predictor that a marriage is going to break down.

Pick your moment carefully to start a delicate discussion. For example, do everything you can to restrain yourself from haranguing him the minute one of you walks in the front door from work. There is no need to take a totally 1950s housewife approach – no one is demanding you fetch his slippers and make dinner first – but there is a happy medium. Like many important things in life, success is largely down to timing.

And here's a newsflash: (most) men are not telepathic. Although we would like them magically to know what it is we want or need, unfortunately and annoyingly this is generally not the case. They need to be informed, out loud, rather than just in your head or to your friends. So, instead of wishing your husband would unload the dishwasher and then spending all evening seething inside when he fails in this task he did not even know he had been set, play fair: it is far more productive simply to ask him, in a studiedly neutral and non-judgemental tone of voice, to do so. Sure, it is incredibly irritating even to have to ask at all – in an ideal world, he would just do it of his own accord – but there it is, that is the world we live in, and asking is still better than having a fight about it.

It is also worth remembering that, for most, arguing becomes infinitely less fulfilling once you're married because it suddenly feels so pointless. What are you going to do? Threaten to dump him, like a teenager? Or, as George Eliot rather more elegantly put it in *Middlemarch* (1874):

> In courtship everything is regarded as provisional and preliminary, and the smallest sample of virtue or accomplishment is taken to

guarantee delightful stores which the broad leisure of marriage will reveal. But the door-sill of marriage once crossed, expectation is concentrated on the present. Having once embarked on your marital voyage, it is impossible not to be aware that you make no way and that the sea is not within sight — that, in fact, you are exploring an enclosed basin.

Almost all arguments between married couples basically deal with the same issues over and over again, just perhaps with a marginally different spin. You might as well simply say 'argument no. 53' and have done with it; you both know the contours of the discussion anyway, as you've had it a million times before. The issues will, in the main, always remain unresolved, so the only sensible path, rather than arguing and arguing about it, is to try to work out a way to agree to disagree. It helps if the issue in question is whether, say, to fly World Traveller or World Traveller Plus rather than more serious issues such as whether or not to have children or where to live.

3. *Be polite to each other*. So many couples are so rude to each other. Don't be. Not only is it horribly undignified; it is also extraordinarily self-destructive. Say 'please' and 'thank you' as often as possible; at dinner parties, at least pretend to be interested in anecdotes you've heard a million times before; be kind and considerate in the same way you are with your friends. (For more on this, see pages 149 [*How To Be Happy Though Married*] and 193 [Top Five Books About Happy Marriages].)

4. *Get the practicalities right*. Never admit you know how to sew, iron or take out the rubbish. If at all possible, have separate bathrooms or at least separate sinks and/or loos, and employ a cleaner (for more on this, see page 151 [The Etiquette of the

Bathroom]). Separate wardrobes are also a boon, if you happen to have money to burn. It is imperative that domestic precedent is established at the very beginning of the marriage. So if you want to implement a policy whereby you both agree to leave your mobile phones by the front door when you get home from work – that is, to prevent either of you answering phone calls or checking emails when you are supposed to be having dinner (or at least watching a DVD) together – then you need to implement this immediately, ideally the day after you get back from honeymoon. Getting married is an opportunity for a new start.

5. *Think of sex the same way you think of exercise.* This particularly applies once you have been married for a while, and once you have children. Research from the Gottman Institute (again) shows the benefits of having sex even when (within limits) you do not necessarily feel like it. Think of it in the same way as you might about forcing yourself to go to the gym even when a night slumped in front of the telly sounds far more appealing. It is good for you and you will feel much better afterwards, so just do it, even if only for health reasons. In all likelihood you'll like it when you actually get down to it; it's just the prospect of it that seems such an effort, especially after a long day at work. Physical affection generally is essential: with all the rigmarole of everyday life, it is amazing and also terrifying how many days can go past without remembering to give one's partner a hug.

6. *Ignore stupid conventions.* All couples are bonkers in their ways and habits, so as long as you're both happy with your collective bonkers-ness, then do not be cowed by what other people think. If you both want to read your books at suppertime, then

great, do it. If you decide you'll both change your surname by deed poll rather than you ditching your maiden name or even going double-barrelled, great, do it: it is perfectly legal. If you want to phone each other a hundred times a day, or conversely if you want to maintain total radio silence until you see each other in the evening, great, do it. If one of you wants to leave a party early, and the other doesn't, great, do it (as long as it is safe for you to get home alone): there is simply no logic to the (strangely prevailing) theory that if one of you can't have fun, neither of you should have fun. It makes no sense. The key thing, whatever the issue, is that you are both in agreement with each other; whether or not you are in agreement with the rest of the world is irrelevant.

7. *It is the little things that matter.* Never underestimate the importance of random acts of kindness. There is infinitely more romance in being unexpectedly brought a cup of tea in bed than in a lifetime of grand gestures.

Now watch and laugh as this fair lady author ends up getting a divorce within the year. Ha.

THE FIRST ANNIVERSARY

THE designated theme for the first wedding anniversary is paper. This seems entirely inappropriate since paper is by its nature flimsy, easily destroyed and at its worst in the rain — not qualities anyone would want in a marriage. But paper it is, so one must make the best of it. A love letter is the obvious choice for a gift; however, since this is probably the only significant anniversary until the Seven Year Itch, it could be argued that it is worth plumping for a present that will last. This is easy for women because so many of us have a secret, lingering stationery fetish, but for men it is rather harder since (to generalize for a second) the sight of a beautifully designed lined notebook from Paris is rather less likely, mysteriously, to throw them into paroxysms of pleasure. You could just find him something on the Viking Direct website, but it might say something about the state of your marriage to gift a stapler. Here, then, are a few paper-themed alternatives.

- A photo album. One made with photo software on your computer is an option because it will look so professional; however, this in some ways defeats the purpose, and there is a rather unsatisfying lack of physicality about these sorts of products that means that making photo albums the old-fashioned way — developing photos and then sticking them in — will always trump it. Even better, how about a scrapbook full of ephemera from the last year: concert programmes, train tickets, restaurant receipts and the like?

- A pornographic origami kit. Yes, they exist, and they are even funnier than they sound, if that's possible.
- An antique book. The best present ever, in any context, for anyone. Go to www.abe.com and browse the works of his favourite author. A battered copy of an old advice book might be fun too, for example, Reverend E. J. Hardy's *How To Be Happy Though Married* (1885) (see page 149).
- Some kind of suitably manly stationery: a Smythson notebook, perhaps, to encourage him to write that novel/screenplay/business plan.
- Frame a photograph of the two of you together. This is a risky enterprise, however, since it is exceptionally hard to achieve without it being naff. As long as there is only one photograph of this sort in your whole house, you can probably get away with it, just about; any more than that is just too narcissistic for words.
- The complete works of his favourite author. Even if this is Stephen King or Patrick O'Brian. This is not the moment to stand in literary judgement.
- A painting, poster, print or drawing. It is time-consuming to find the perfect choice, but you'll have such fun searching and it will be not only a brilliant present but also a great investment.
- A board game, if that's his and/or your thing.
- A Taschen book. Though you may have to sell your house to pay for it.
- Stalk eBay for ephemera like old letters, pamphlets or postcards. Pick a subject such as his field of work or his favourite band, and go from there.
- Does he have even the slightest interest in drawing or painting? A set of art stuff – paper, paints, an easel, etc. – to encourage a latent talent.

TOP FIVE BOOKS ABOUT HAPPY MARRIAGES

WHILE stories of unhappy marriages are a staple of great litera-
ture, books about happy marriages are astonishingly scarce.
Without conflict, the fear is that the reader will fall asleep drib-
bling from boredom. Below, however, are five books with which
there is not even the tiniest risk of this — not even a yawn.

DENIS MACKAIL, *GREENERY STREET* (1925)

Greenery Street is an account of the first year of Ian and Felicity
Jackson's marriage as they move into a new house on a street in
Chelsea that is populated almost entirely by newly-weds like
them. After that, not much happens; rather, it is about the
small, everyday trials and tribulations that everyone in this
situation experiences.

> It is the first, magical year. Every day, every hour has almost its
> separate thrill. The purchase of a new galvanized-iron dustbin
> moves us to the marrow, triumph over a tradesman raises us to
> undreamt-of height, defeat by the Inspector of Taxes plunges us
> into bottomless depths. Everything is new, everything is exciting,
> and every excitement is doubled by the fact that it is shared . . . Aren't
> there two of us now to face and outface the whole world? But if you
> think we're going to let anybody else in on our latest secret, then
> you're pretty completely mistaken. You laughed when we told you
> about the tradesman; you yawned when we boasted of our new
> dustbin. Very well, then; we've got a much bigger affair than either
> of those up our sleeves, but we're not going to waste it on you.

These days, there are not many of us who are moved to the marrow by the purchase of a new bin, but episodes like this are precisely part of the novel's charm. It veers between utterly sentimental tosh and comically practical musings, all within a single page. Almost every chapter culminates in Ian and Felicity rapturously embracing one another following some minor tiff about a domestic matter. It is a sweet, touching and deceptively unusual portrayal of one couple just beginning to navigate their way through married life, and is truly unlike any other novel out there.

HANS FALLADA, *LITTLE MAN, WHAT NOW?* (1932)

This brilliant novel (not to be confused with Morrissey's song of the same name, which he borrowed from it) by the author of the more famous *Alone in Berlin* follows newly-weds Johannes Pinnenberg, a bookkeeper, and his wife, Emma, as they negotiate the economic hardships of Germany in the early 1930s.

> From a distance a marriage looks so extraordinarily easy: two people marry and have children. They live together, are as nice as possible to each other, and try to get on with life. Friendship, love, kindliness, food, drink, sleep, going to work, housekeeping, an outing on a Sunday, occasionally a visit to the cinema in the evening! And that's it.
>
> But close up, the whole business dissolves into a thousand individual problems. The marriage itself recedes into the background; it is taken for granted and is simply the precondition for the rest. But what about the casserole? And should he tell Mrs Scharrenhofer this very evening to take the clock out of the room? That's the reality.

It was a huge best-seller when it was first published.

ANTONIA FRASER, *MUST YOU GO? MY LIFE WITH HAROLD PINTER* (2010)

If you can get past all the pass-the-sick-bag name-dropping that is sprinkled throughout the book, you will find this an almost unbearably moving account of Antonia Fraser's 33-year-long relationship with Harold Pinter. 'I first saw Harold', she remembers, 'across a crowded room, but it was lunchtime, not some enchanted evening, and we did not speak.' The marriage seems to have been a profoundly happy one — 'to the infinite degree happy beyond all possible expectations', in Fraser's words — which really is rare to read about, especially in a memoir. He used to write her incredibly touching poems: 'I shall miss you so much when I'm dead' begins one he composed when he was diagnosed with a terminal illness. And at the end, when she writes about the moment he died, you will sob as you have seldom sobbed before.

LAURIE COLWIN, *HAPPY ALL THE TIME* (1978)

Guido and Vincent are third cousins, both living in Cambridge, Massachusetts, and then later New York. They pursue, and then marry, an unusual pair of women: Holly and Misty. That's pretty much the entire plot. These are funny, unusual characters who are neither types nor clichés, but the story of the small dramas of their existence is immensely interesting and stimulating, with the occasional wise gem thrown in, for example:

> What was the use of discussion? Holly simply went her own way, and if her way was not Guido's, Guido reminded himself that he was not married to his double.

Or this, on the subject of weddings:

> [Vincent] felt their love was quite rich enough to do without any ornamentation.

Colwin also raises a number of discussion points about marriage. These include: love is great but takes work; forming a relationship with one's friend's partners is a minefield of its own; and people often unconsciously try to sabotage their own happiness, as articulated here:

> [Guido] looked up to find Holly standing meekly in a doorway, carrying coffee cups on a tray.
>
> 'I'm sorry,' she said. 'Sometimes everything is so smooth and invisible that I can't see it without discord.'

Picking a fight, it's called.

NANCY MITFORD, *THE PURSUIT OF LOVE* (1945)

And so we find ourselves with yet another excuse to bang on about this most perfect of novels. First of all, here is what Fanny, the narrator, has to say about her own marriage:

> . . . I became happily engaged to Alfred Wincham, then a young don at, now Warden of, St. Peter's College, Oxford. With this kindly scholarly man I have been perfectly happy ever since, finding in our home at Oxford that refuge from the storms and puzzles of life which I had always wanted.

And that is all. Nothing more. The rest of the book is less about the everyday banality of marriage itself than about why we end up with whom we end up with. It is indeed frequently a complete mystery to onlookers as a bride stumbles blindly up the aisle towards her groom, but of course that thing we call 'love' is actually such a complicated combination of chemicals, baggage, practicalities, background, etc. that it can be hard for outsiders to understand. Here are some of Mitford's suggestions as to how and why the characters in her novel make this most momentous of decisions:

Of Louisa's marriage to Lord Fort William

She was in heaven at the prospect of getting away from [the family home] Alconleigh for ever.

Of Linda's marriage to Tony Koenig

Tony, in those days, and to unsophisticated country girls like us, seemed a glorious and glamorous creature. When we first saw him, at Linda's and my coming-out ball, he was in his last year at Oxford, a member of Bullingdon, a splendid young man with a Rolls-Royce, plenty of beautiful horses, exquisite clothes, and large luxurious rooms, where he entertained on a lavish scale. In person he was tall and fair, on the heavy side, but with a well-proportioned figure; he had already a faint touch of pomposity, a thing which Linda had never come across before, and which she found not unattractive. She took him, in short, at his own valuation.

Of Linda's fleeting affair with Communist radical journalist Christian

Linda was a plum ripe for shaking . . . Intelligent and energetic, but with no outlet for her energies, unhappy in her marriage, uninterested in her child, and inwardly oppressed with a sense of futility, she was in the mood either to take up some cause, or to embark upon a love affair. That a cause should now be presented by an attractive young man made both it and him irresistible.

Of Linda's great romance with French aristocrat Fabrice

She was filled with a strange, wild, unfamiliar happiness, and knew that this was love.

In the way of true, profound, storybook, Romeo-and-Juliet-style love that you are lucky if you experience even once in a lifetime, Linda finds it impossible to offer up a laundry list of the reasons why she loved him. She just did.

And at the end of all these romantic shenanigans, what have we learnt from Mitford? What, in her view, is the key to a successful marriage, regardless of the actual feelings of the participants towards each other? 'Very very great niceness — *gentillesse* — and wonderful good manners.' Enough said.

PERMISSIONS

Lines from Dylan Thomas's *Under Milk Wood*, published by Orion, are reproduced by permission of David Higham Associates.

Extracts from works by Nancy Mitford are copyright © 1945 Nancy Mitford. Reproduced by permission of the Estate of Nancy Mitford, c/o Rogers, Coleridge and White Ltd.

Beds Buying Guide is copyright © johnlewis.com, and reproduced by permission.

Extracts from *The Winds of Heaven* by Monica Dickens (1955) and *Greenery Street* by Denis Mackail (1925), are reproduced by kind permission of Persephone Books.

Extract from www.farrow-ball.com is copyright © Farrow&Ball and reproduced by kind permission.

'Poem ('To A)' taken from *Collected Poems and Prose* copyright © Estate of Harold Pinter and reprinted by permission of Faber and Faber Ltd.

Lines from *Must You Go? My Life with Harold Pinter* by Antonia Fraser copyright © Antonia Fraser 2010 and reproduced by kind permission of Orion Books.

A NOTE ON THE TYPE

MRS Eaves is a transitional serif typeface designed by Zuzana Licko in 1996, and licensed by Emigre, a typefoundry run by Licko and her husband Rudy VanderLans. Mrs Eaves is a revival of a 1757 type designed by English printer John Baskerville, and is related to contemporary Baskerville typefaces.

Like Baskerville, Mrs Eaves has a near-vertical stress. Identifying characters include the lowercase g with its open lower counter and swash-like ear; the uppercase Q with its flowing swash-like tail; the uppercase C with its serifs at top and bottom; and the uppercase G with its sharp spur suggesting a vestigial serif.

Mrs Eaves is named after Sarah Eaves, who was Baskerville's housekeeper. When she and her five children were abandoned by Mr Eaves, she and Baskerville got together, working side by side and eventually marrying when the estranged husband died. Like the widows of Caslon, Bodoni, and the daughters of Fournier, Sarah completed the printing of the unfinished volumes that John Baskerville left upon his death. The name 'Mrs Eaves' honours one of the forgotten wives in the history of typography.

ALSO AVAILABLE BY FRANCESCA BEAUMAN

HOW TO CRACK AN EGG WITH ONE HAND

A Pocket Book for the New Mother

In *How to Crack an Egg with One Hand,* Francesca Beauman has handily compiled everything you need to know (and a few things you don't) in order to embark on the mindboggling journey that is modern motherhood. As well as offering her own humorous yet pertinent advice on everything from what a new mother ought to wear on the red carpet to the best books to read while feeding a baby, Beauman has also tracked down what Mark Twain had to say on teething, Vladimir Nabakov on prams, Mrs Gaskell on six-month-olds and Mrs Beeton on breastfeeding.

From the totally frivolous to the deeply serious, from the cultural to the historical, from the history of the caesarean to celebrity baby names, this is an intelligent, classy and eclectic guide for every twenty-first-century mother or mother-to-be. For it is important to acknowledge that, even though they may have a basketball in their stomachs, they still have a brain in their heads. It is a book to give to friends, daughters and sisters – and to cherish for yourself. True, you may not ever *need* to know what year the epidural was invented, how to ~~write your child's name in Chinese, or what~~ the gestational period of an anteater is, but isn't it fabulous that you do?

ORDER BY PHONE: +44 (0)1256 302 699; BY EMAIL: DIRECT@MACMILLAN.CO.UK

DELIVERY IS USUALLY 3–5 WORKING DAYS. FREE POSTAGE AND PACKAGING FOR ORDERS OVER £20.

ONLINE: WWW.BLOOMSBURY.COM/BOOKSHOP

PRICES AND AVAILABILITY SUBJECT TO CHANGE WITHOUT NOTICE.

WWW.BLOOMSBURY.COM

BLOOMSBURY